THE
WORLD
Jesus
KNEW

THE
WORLD
Jesus
KNEW

Seth Pollinger, Ph.D.
General Editor
with Randy Southern

WORTHY
PUBLISHING

museum of the Bible
BOOKS

THE WORLD JESUS KNEW
Copyright © 2017 by MUSEUM OF THE BIBLE, INC.

Published by Worthy Books, an imprint of Worthy Publishing Group, a division of Worthy Media, Inc., One Franklin Park, 6100 Tower Circle, Suite 210, Franklin, TN 37067, in association with Museum of the Bible.

WORTHY is a registered trademark of Worthy Media, Inc.

HELPING PEOPLE EXPERIENCE THE HEART OF GOD

eBook available wherever digital books are sold.

_____

Library of Congress CIP data is on file.

_____

Produced with the assistance of Hudson Bible (www.HudsonBible.com)

ISBN: 978-1-94547-007-3

Cover Design: Matt Smartt, Smartt Guys design

Cover Image: Whiteway/Istockphoto

Printed in the United States of America

17 18 19 20 21 LBM 8 7 6 5 4 3 2 1

Contents

About This Book

*T*he *World Jesus Knew* is a fictional account set during the last week of Jesus's earthly life as recounted in the Bible. The story begins with his triumphal entry into Jerusalem and concludes with his resurrection. Oddly enough, Jesus remains a minor character in this portrayal, as he is seen from the perspectives of various other people. Yet it is an account based, as much as possible, on reliable information about first-century Jewish and Roman history and culture. The author has attempted to condense such relevant information and include it in the brief openings of each chapter.

The events of the story take place somewhere around AD 33 in Jerusalem. Judea is under the jurisdiction of the Roman Empire, a fact that causes consternation, irritation, and sometimes full-fledged outrage among Jewish citizens. Also troubling to many of them is the suspicion that their religious leaders are forming political alliances with the Romans, and perhaps sacrificing the integrity of their law in the process.

In addition to Jesus, other significant biblical and historic characters in this story include four of his disciples (Simon Peter, the other Simon, John, and Judas Iscariot); Lazarus; the high priest at the time (Caiaphas) and his father-in-law (Annas);

Pontius Pilate; and Herod. Peter's mother-in-law is mentioned in the Bible, but not by name. Here she is called Miriam.

Fictional characters whose stories are interwoven with these characters include Eli (a self-serving priest), Jared and his brothers (in Jerusalem for Passover), Uri (an older man who becomes something of a mentor to Jared), and Chana (a new follower of Jesus). These characters are not found in Bible dictionaries or history books, yet they are intended to reflect similar people who lived and likely had similar mindsets and motivations.

To aid the reader's understanding of the world's culture of Jesus's day, brief introductions precede each chapter. These introductions spotlight a different topic (such as the role of women, trade and commerce, or religious practices) for each chapter. They compare, contrast, and connect events that were occurring in Israel with events that were happening in other cultures and nations around the world at the time of Jesus.

Near the end of the Bible's book of John we read: "Jesus did many other things as well. If every one of them were written down, I suppose that even the whole world would not have room for the books that would be written" (John 21:25). This book is not meant to comprehensively cover the life of Jesus. Yet here the reader will find much to ponder between the various perspectives, the behind-the-scenes glimpses, and the opportunity to get a first-person perspective of the world that Jesus knew.

Chapter 1

The Politics Jesus Knew

ISRAEL'S PLACE IN THE MIDDLE EAST IN 1ST CENTURY AD

The Israel in which Jesus lived and ministered was a far cry from the conquering nation that cut a wide swath through Canaan under the military leadership of Joshua. Likewise, the golden years of Israel's monarchy—the reigns of David and Solomon— were but a page from history in Jesus's day.

In 587 BC, the Babylonians, led by King Nebuchadnezzar, laid waste to Jerusalem and destroyed the magnificent temple that Solomon had built. Nebuchadnezzar's army exiled the people of Israel to Babylon.

That defeat proved to be pivotal for Israel. After the Babylonian captivity ended around 538 BC, a succession of empires assumed control. The Persians ruled the land until 333 BC, when the Greeks, led by Alexander the Great, conquered it. The descendents of Alexander fought over regional control and were relatively benign conquerors. At times, Jews were allowed to rule their own affairs.

Jewish self-rule ended in 63 BC, when the Roman general Pompey conquered Israel and absorbed the land of Palestine into the Roman Empire. Rome appointed its own rulers over Israel and maintained a pervasive military presence in the region to discourage rebellion.

Despite the Romans' oppressive presence in Israel, the Roman government gave the local Jewish leaders limited freedom to work out their own religious disputes and affairs. Some Jewish people looked to the priests and teachers of the Law for guidance not only in religious matters, but in social, legal, and political matters as well.

In order to maintain their political position, the Jewish leaders had to strike a delicate balance. Some felt they had to cooperate with Roman authorities without giving the appearance of cooperation. Others wanted to fight. Still others abhorred Rome but were looking for a solution that didn't involve physical conflict. The leaders of Israel often compromised the best interests of Israel to ensure the peace that the Romans required of their conquered territories.

Rome's demand for compliance put pressure on local rulers to keep a close watch on Jesus and his followers. Different factions tried to prevent any social movement that could get out of control (and would also threaten local balance among religious leaders). The leaders all struggled with how to appease Rome, and they drew the line in various places. It was a power struggle where the goal, for many, was to keep their own power.

Eli snaked his way through the crowd gathered in the courtyard of a house in the village of Bethany. The house was small compared to others in which Eli had heard Jesus speak. Two doors were cut into the mudbrick walls of the courtyard. One led to a storage area for tools and equipment; the other led to a larger storage area for animals.

Eli kept his arms folded into his chest as he moved through the assembled throng. He knew from past experience that many of the people who gathered outside Jesus's teaching engagements did not come only to hear him speak. Many came to be healed of all manner of . . . afflictions. Eli shuddered. The realization that he might be pushing past someone who was possessed by a demon or suffering from a blood disorder caused him to pull his arms more tightly to his body.

He climbed seven steep stairs to a landing. The door at the top of the stairs was blocked by a group of men jostling for position. Eli opted for a less-populated spot near a window just to the left of the men. Unfortunately, Jesus and his disciples were on the opposite side of the room. Eli could see everything that was happening, but he couldn't hear anything but murmurs.

He grabbed the windowsill, squeezed his body against the wall, and turned his ear to the opening, hoping to hear more. "Whose house is this?" he whispered to the man next to him.

"Jesus is staying at the home of Simon," the man replied, "the leper who was cured by his power."

Eli immediately let go of the sill and took a step back from the house. "A leper!" he exclaimed in disgust. He held his hands out as if they had been contaminated. The disease itself was bad enough. Even worse, though, was the ritual impurity it created, forcing isolation from friends, family, and public worship. It was a loathsome condition that generated fear in many Jews.

"Do not concern yourself," the man replied. "Simon has been made clean by Jesus." The man placed his own hand on the wall to demonstrate his point.

Eli regarded him warily and then turned his attention back to the house. Inside, nearly two dozen people filled the small central living area. The interior was dark. Several oil lamps, strategically positioned throughout the room, cast odd-angled shadows on all four walls. The sunlight that filtered through the windows was obscured by the figures of those, like Eli, who crowded into their openings.

The feast was over, though a few people were still reclining at the table. Others were milling about, talking with one another and with some of Jesus's disciples. The rest were gathered around the teacher from Nazareth—or so Eli assumed. From his vantage point, he couldn't actually see Jesus in their midst.

He noticed that several people in the room were pointing to and staring at a man who stood near two women.

"How healthy Lazarus looks for one who spent four days in the tomb," the man next to Eli said.

Lazarus.

Eli turned and scanned the crowd in the courtyard, looking for two men who would be doing their best to remain inconspicuous. He did not see them.

They will be near the front door.

Before he left the window, a movement inside the house caught his eye. The crowd parted and Eli could see Jesus seated near the table. One of the women who had been talk-ing with the disciples picked up a large jar and approached Jesus. She knelt before the teacher and poured the jar's oily contents over his feet. A wave of excitement rolled through the room as the smell of perfume—very *expensive* perfume, Eli noted—filled the air.

One of the disciples—the treasurer, the one known as Judas Iscariot—stepped forward. With forceful gestures, he pointed to the woman and then to the empty jar. His voice was lost in the din, but his displeasure was definitely not. The woman kept her back to Eli. Still on her knees, she was using her long hair to wipe the oil from Jesus's feet.

Jesus held up his hand to calm his outraged disciple. He gestured toward the woman in a way that, even from a dis-tance, left no doubt as to his approval of her. The rebuked disciple stormed from the house.

Eli gave a moment's thought to going after him, but he had a more pressing matter to attend to—one that he would surely have to explain later. He left the window and hurried through the crowd to the front door, where some of the guests were starting to emerge. Lazarus was not yet one of them.

Eli spotted the two men he sought standing in the street, facing Simon's house. The crowd had parted in such a way that the guests leaving the feast had to walk past the men. Eli joined the line of people filing out of the house.

Ahead of him, the two men shifted their stance and stared intently at the departing guests. Each one had slipped his right hand inside his cloak, at chest level, and held it there. Eli carefully approached the men.

They failed to notice him at first, focused as they were on Simon's front door. A quick wave of his hand finally caught their attention. Their eyes went wide when they recognized Eli—so wide, in fact, that he felt compelled to look around to see if anyone else had noticed. He glanced back at the men, gestured to their concealed hands, and then shook his head once in a deliberately exaggerated movement.

The two men looked at each other and then back at Eli. He met their confused glances with another shake of his head—a confirmation of his previous gesture. The men removed their hands from their cloaks. Sunlight briefly glinted off the handle of a concealed weapon as one of the men pulled his outer garment closed again.

Muttering their frustration, the two men walked away quickly, pausing to look back only when shouts of "Lazarus! Lazarus!" erupted from the crowd. The brother of Mary and Martha—the second most popular person in Bethany that day—returned to his home unharmed, without an inkling of how close he had come to death a second time.

Eli stopped a couple who were walking away from Simon's house. "Did the teacher reveal where he plans to go after he leaves Bethany?"

The woman smiled broadly. "Last night two of his disciples were guests in our home. During the evening meal they told us—"

Eli fixed the woman with a cold glare that stopped her in midsentence. Her smile vanished and she took a step backward.

"His disciples revealed to us that Jesus will depart for Jerusalem tomorrow," her husband continued as he stepped in front of her. He was clearly more intimidated than his wife by this interrogation from a stranger. His cheeks and forehead burned bright red as he cast his eyes downward. Eli shook his head and brushed past the two of them.

The walk to Jerusalem—a distance of less than two miles—exceeded the limits of a Sabbath's journey. According to the oral traditions of the Pharisees, Eli was forbidden to make the trip until morning. He stayed with his companions in Bethany another night.

A morning haze burned off quickly as Eli made his way down the southeastern slope of the Mount of Olives to Jerusalem. Near the village of Bethpage, he saw two men emerge from a house near the road. They stood for a moment, discussing something. One of the men pointed toward Jerusalem. The other shrugged his shoulders. They turned in unison and began walking in Eli's direction—back toward Bethany. They did not hurry, but there was a purpose in their gait.

As they drew closer, Eli recognized them as two of Jesus's disciples. He could not recall either man's name.

"Peace be with you!" he called out. If either man returned his greeting, Eli did not hear him. The breach of etiquette bothered him but did not deter him. "I see you are out early this morning, diligently working on behalf of the teacher we all follow."

The two men slowed their pace but did not stop as they approached him. "Are we not always doing the work of our teacher?" one of them replied.

"Indeed!" Eli agreed with a vigorous nod. "Indeed we are. May I assist you in preparing for the teacher's journey to Jerusalem today?"

Eli hid a smile with the back of his hand as the disciples exchanged glances. He wondered if these were the two men who had stayed with the couple in Bethany.

"The arrangements for Jesus's journey have already been made," the taller of the two replied. "We require no further assistance." His tone was cordial but firm, so Eli bade the men farewell and continued on his way. He had other ways of gathering information for his associates.

As Eli neared the house from which they had come, he glanced over his shoulder. Jesus's disciples had disappeared around a bend on their way back to Bethany. He took a deep breath and approached the door.

"Peace be with everyone who dwells within these walls!" he called.

The door opened and an old man limped out. He leaned heavily on a carved staff as he walked. "Peace be with you, young man," he replied.

"Sir, I have been sent to your home by my master, the teacher—Jesus of Nazareth," Eli explained.

"What *more* does your master require of me?" the man asked. He did not try to disguise the annoyance in his voice.

Eli waved his hands and shook his head. "No, no," he insisted. "He asks nothing more of you. I am here because the servants he sent to your door have proved untrustworthy. The teacher has sent me to make certain that his requests have been clearly stated and granted."

"They have," the old man told him. He raised his staff and pointed it at Eli. "Now you tell me: Will your master prove *himself* to be trustworthy? Will he swear to me that my donkey will be returned after it has carried him to Jerusalem?"

"A donkey?"

Eli nodded. Caiaphas, the high priest of Israel, considered Eli's words for a moment. Then he, too, nodded slowly, as did a dozen other priests, scribes, and elders who had quickly assembled in the large reception area of Caiaphas's palace to hear Eli's report. The significance—the *audacity*—of the image of a donkey was not lost on anyone as familiar as they were with the prophecy of Zechariah. The general population might not be educated enough to associate a donkey with the anticipated arrival of the Messiah, but this group certainly was.

"After calling Lazarus from the tomb, does he now presume himself a king?" one priest asked.

"The whole world is running after him!" another noted.

"Long have we endured the blasphemies of this man," Caiaphas said. "For almost three years have we witnessed his callous disregard for the oral traditions of our people."

"For three years have we been made to look foolish by his parables and teachings," a scribe added.

"Yet now his own pride and lust for power makes itself known," Caiaphas continued. "We must devise a plan that will make the Romans take notice and quiet his opposition to our leadership."

"So it shall be left to . . . the *Romans* to do what the Law requires—to put this blasphemer to death?" one the elders asked.

"How long must we be forced to live with these brutal leaders?" another priest muttered.

"The day will come when we will be freed from their tyranny," Caiaphas replied. "Until that time, even brutal leaders can be made useful. They may rid us of an insidious enemy."

Eli gazed at the faces of the men gathered in the room—among them the most powerful Jewish leaders in all of Israel. A surge of pride swelled within him. They had gathered here because of news that *he* had delivered . . . news acquired through stealth and subterfuge. Modesty did not prevent him from believing that one day these men would regard him as an equal.

His moment of triumph was short-lived.

"And now you must answer for your actions in Bethany last night," Caiaphas said. The chief priest had spoken with his back turned to Eli. For a moment Eli wondered if the chief priest's words could have been directed at him. When everyone else turned to look at him, his suspicion was confirmed.

"Our *servants* informed us that you brought attention to them and prevented them from carrying out their assigned task as Lazarus left the house."

Eli held his ground. "Forgive me, Caiaphas, but those servants were sent to kill a man who had been brought back to life once already. What if Jesus had . . ."

Eli stopped before he said, ". . . raised him a second time." He realized his thoughtless words gave the Nazarene too much credit. But it was already too late. Caiaphas thundered, "They were sent to kill a man who claimed to have been raised from the dead! What reason had you to interfere with his just punishment? As long as Lazarus is walking around, he persuades gullible people that this Jesus is someone who can challenge our authority!"

Eli closed his eyes and held up one hand. "The *intent* of my words was clear," he insisted. "We must be careful. We can't risk giving this blasphemer any more opportunities to make us look weak and foolish."

Caiaphas paced at the edge of the room. He stared out the window at the upper courtyard, where the remnants of a bonfire still smoldered. After several moments of contemplation, he stood next to Eli and addressed the group of men. "Our young priest does not yet understand the importance of speaking precisely. However, in this matter he has shown wisdom. We no longer need to provoke this blasphemer from Nazareth. He will deliver himself into our hands with his words and deeds. Soon all of Jerusalem will know of his blasphemy. We need only to continue to keep a close watch on this man who has escaped our traps for three years."

The high priest placed his hand on Eli's shoulder. "Jesus of Nazareth will soon give us just cause to act. And when he does, we will act swiftly. The teacher will be in our hands before his followers realize he has been taken from them."

"How soon does this man plan to make his entrance into Jerusalem?" one of the other priests asked.

The roar of a crowd near the eastern gate of the city answered his question.

Chapter 2

The Empire Jesus Knew

THE ROMAN EMPIRE IN 1ST CENTURY AD

The thirty-three years of Jesus's life coincided with the rise of the Roman Empire as it expanded in its power and influence. At its apex, the Empire comprised forty-eight modern countries. Its northern boundary lay in modern Scotland, its southern boundary in North Africa. From west to east, the empire stretched across Europe and into Asia—all the way to the modern border between Iraq and Iran. The extraordinary Roman road system, which extended across the Empire, connected the world in a way never before possible. The intricately planned thoroughfares made long-distance travel safer, faster, and more convenient. The world Jesus knew was rapidly becoming smaller.

In time, the region of Judea, in which Jerusalem and its surrounding areas were located, was established as a "client kingdom" of Rome. Herod the Great, a half-Jew, ruled as a Jewish king but lived his life very much like a Roman. He was not governor of Jerusalem; the Roman governor lived in Caesarea. The Jewish people were not fooled by his title. They recognized that, ultimately, Herod had to answer to Rome.

Following Herod's death, Israel was governed by a combination of Herod's sons and Roman officials, including Pontius Pilate. The concept of Pax Romana gave conquered territories some degree of autonomy, but the paganism of the

Romans and the monotheism of the Jews were on a collision course from day one. Add to that the tax burdens that Rome placed on Israel, and it's not difficult to pinpoint the roots of rebellion among certain factions of the Jewish people.

After centuries of struggling with foreign rulers, many Jews debated about how they could throw off the shackles of Rome and live in independence. They remembered a century and a half earlier when the Greek Empire and its vile ruler, Antiochus (IV) Epiphanes, had pushed them too far in attempting to corrupt their worship habits and absorb them into a worldwide Hellenistic society. Outraged Jewish dissidents had organized and eventually defeated the Seleucid army, regaining their freedom and enabling them to cleanse the Temple. Was that the response they should take now, against the despised Romans? A great dispute occurred along a spectrum—some advocated revolt, others flight to the desert, while others chose compliance.

"How long will we wait before we seek out a hostel?"
The town square of Jerusalem was bustling four days before Passover. Pilgrims from throughout Israel packed the marketplace to fulfill their ritual obligation to spend the money they made from selling their firstfruits. They bought meat, fish, leeks, dried fruit, nuts, and wine sweetened with honey. Others attended pottery workshops where artisans created cooking pots and other things.

Noam, Jared, and Seth—brothers from the city of Tyre, over 100 miles north of Jerusalem—stood with dozens of other travelers in the center of the activity. The travelers stood apart from each other in groups: a husband and wife here, a family of four there. A few groups numbered more than a dozen, and many men stood alone, but as far as Jared could see, he and his brothers were the only trio. His older brother, Noam, carried a large pack that contained, among other things, the brothers' Passover clothing—the whitest garments they owned. His younger brother, Seth, the one who had posed the question, held a hemp rope tethered to a lamb whose appearance had no blemish or defect.

Jared started to answer Seth when a tall man, dressed in a purple cloak, approached. Behind him, several onlookers stared openly at his attire. Purple garments were rarities in the villages and towns from which many of them came.

"You are weary from your travels," the man said in a loud voice. "I welcome you as guests to my home. You will share our Passover table. You will eat your fill of our food and drink your fill of our wine. You will sleep in our guest room on our roof."

Jared bowed his head to the man. "My brothers and I—"

"Peace be to you and everyone who dwells in your house," came a voice from behind him. The tall man brushed past Jared and approached the largest group of travelers, who appeared to be a three-generation family made up of some fifteen adults and children. The family's patriarch bowed low to the approaching host and continued his greeting. "We would be honored to share the Passover in your home."

The tall man signaled to four servants who stood nearby. The servants gathered the family's belongings, including their own lamb, and led the group away. The tall man continued on to the marketplace.

Jared watched the servants and large family leave. When he turned around, he saw several other travelers talking with potential hosts. Many of the men who had been standing alone were already gone.

His brothers were no longer looking at their fellow travelers. They were staring at a crowd just east of their present position. Jared could tell from their clinched jaws that they didn't like what they saw. The knot in his stomach tightened as he followed their gaze.

Even with the morning sun shining in his eyes, Jared had no trouble spotting the source of his brothers' concern. The sea of Jerusalem's citizens and visitors—so dense in some places that people had trouble passing—had parted like the Red Sea waters before Moses. Through its middle ran a fast-moving river of red.

"It's a small squad," Noam noted just loudly enough for his brothers to hear, "perhaps two *contubernia*." Seth slipped his hand under his cloak and removed a dagger from a sheath that hung near his right hip. With a quick flick of his wrist, he positioned the flat part of the blade against his inner forearm. A casual observer would be unable to tell that he was armed.

Before the brothers could discuss their next move, an elderly man stepped into their line of vision. The shock of white hair protruding from his head at a variety of angles contrasted sharply with his more traditional-looking beard.

"They are on a routine patrol," the man said. He, too, spoke just loudly enough for the three brothers to hear. "I'll wager that their orders are simply to make their presence known in the midst of so great a crowd."

"They make their presence known to remind us that even during our holy feasts, we are to serve the Roman Empire," Seth replied boldly. He punctuated his sentence by spitting on the ground.

"You will gain nothing by drawing your blade in anger," the old man insisted. "You will only cause trouble and Roman attention. If one of you even raises your hand to them, they will arrest—and kill—all of you."

Seth was surprised that the old man had detected his weapon, but was not swayed by his warning. "Would you have us cower before these dogs?" he asked.

The squadron of Roman soldiers was getting closer. The man reasoned, "Do your plans include hanging from a Roman cross before the Passover celebration has ended? Because that is surely where you will be if you make yourselves known as a threat."

The Roman patrol carved a path through the crowd, straight toward Jared and his brothers. Each soldier wore a linen tunic, bright red from madder dye and girded at a precise length to indicate his rank. Each tunic was cinched with a belt from which hung a dagger and an apron made of strips of leather studded with metal. Their aprons were decorated with tokens and small discs that represented various campaigns in which the soldiers had fought.

The soldiers also wore leg wrappings, strips of material that encircled their lower legs from calves to ankles. They wore socks without toes or heels and leather sandals with iron hobnails. Their round helmets were made of bronze, each featuring a small knob on top, a plate that extended horizontally from the back to protect the neck, and two cheek plates that hung vertically to protect the sides of the head.

The crowded conditions of Jerusalem's streets did not allow the squadrons to march in formation. Still, the soldiers managed to walk in step. The two officers who led the squads, the *decani*, kept their gaze focused on the horizon. They did not acknowledge the thousands of Israelites on all sides of them.

In contrast, the soldiers walking behind the officers cast their gazes in every direction. Some scanned the crowd as though they were looking for specific individuals—perhaps insurrectionists whose faces were familiar to them. Others seemed to monitor the crowd's movements, perhaps looking for potential riots. Still others made eye contact with the people they passed, staring them into submission, daring them to make a rash move or even offer a defiant gaze in return.

Many Jewish children were taught from an early age to lower their heads and avert their eyes when they encountered

Roman soldiers. Jared and his brothers were not among them. They had more reason than most to despise the forces of Rome.

The brothers stared hard at the approaching Roman troops.

"I have but a modest home to offer, but you and your companions would honor me with your presence." The white-haired man was persistent. He stepped slightly to his left to block Jared's view of the soldiers. "Or are these your brothers? I notice that you are sharing a sacrificial lamb."

"What? Yes . . . brothers. We are three brothers from Tyre."

The thunderous clatter of footsteps grew louder. Jared tried to look past the old man, but the man stepped closer to him. "My name is Uri." There was gravitas—and a hint of righteous anger—in his voice now. "I have asked you to share Passover in my home. All I ask in return is that you show me the respect of looking at me as I speak to you."

Jared heard the voice of his father in Uri's words. Apparently, so did his brothers. All three turned immediately to face Uri. Their hardened stares softened considerably.

"Forgive us," Noam said. "We would be honored to share Passover in your home."

While he spoke, the contingent of Roman soldiers marched past, close enough for the brothers to reach out and touch. If any of the soldiers looked in their direction, the brothers didn't notice. When the Romans were out of sight, Uri reached out and patted Seth on the right arm—the one in which he still held the dagger. "There is a time and a season for everything," Uri said. "Follow me."

Uri's house was less than a mile from the temple, but getting there proved to be a challenge. Twice the brothers lost sight of their host in the crowd. Jared was familiar with the city, so he took note of the landmarks and turns along the way so that he would be able to find the old man's house again.

Uri's house was built around a central open court. The small rooms of the structure all opened onto the court, one of which served as an animal pen. That's where Noam tied the brothers' Passover lamb.

"Do you live alone?" Jared asked their host as he led them up a flight of stairs to the roof.

"Yes," Uri replied. "My wife is dead and my children are grown, but I have companions who will join us for the Passover meal. You will find that you have much in common with them." His voice changed ever so slightly as he spoke the final sentence. It was a tone not unlike that of a parent about to surprise a small child with a toy or sweet treat.

"But you hardly know us," Seth protested. "Are your companions—?"

A commotion from the street below interrupted Seth's question. Jared and his brothers ran to the edge of the roof in time to see a wave of people rushing toward the east gate of the city. Shouts of what sounded like joy rose from their midst. The only words the brothers could make out came from a woman directly below them who could not contain her excitement. She stopped long enough to grab the arms of another woman and exclaim, "He is coming!"

Jared looked at Uri, who shrugged. The brothers hesitated for a moment. Uri smiled and nodded toward the stairs.

"Go see for yourself what this is. I suspect you will not rest until you do."

Jared led the way down the stairs, out the front door, and into the street. Up close, the crowd making its way to the east gate seemed even bigger. The crowd's roar from the vicinity of the gate roused the brothers into a run. The street on which they ran intersected the East Gate Road. The sight that greeted them when they reached the intersection stunned and confused all three of them.

Thousands of people were lined up on either side of the East Gate Road. Men were perched in the palm trees beside the thoroughfare. They tore giant leaves from the trees and dropped them to the ground. Men, women, and children gathered the leaves and placed them on the road. Several people in the crowd placed their cloaks on the road as well.

"Hosanna to the Son of David!" someone in the crowd shouted.

"Blessed is he who comes in the name of the Lord!" added another.

Jared nudged the man next to him and asked, "Who is this?"

"This is the prophet Jesus, from Nazareth of Galilee," the man answered.

Jared and Seth turned to Noam. "Jesus of Nazareth?" Jared asked. "Is this not the man you saw in Capernaum . . . the one you said spoke in riddles not even his disciples could understand . . . the one who taught people to love their enemies?"

"Yes, you said he discouraged fighting against Rome, saying that we should 'turn the other cheek' to our enemies," Seth added.

"I reported to you what I saw and heard!" Noam protested. "I defy any man to tell me that there was *anything* in this Nazarene's appearance or words in Capernaum that suggested he would one day be greeted in this manner!"

Jared and his brothers had to elbow their way to the front to see the man riding slowly toward the city. Behind the man, a dozen or so followers on foot took in the spectacle. Most wore looks of astonishment. Others were laughing and pointing at people in the crowd. A few seemed genuinely unsettled by the greeting.

From a distance, the man on the donkey betrayed little emotion. Yet as he passed by the brothers, Jared noticed that even as he affirmed the excitement of the crowd, he appeared more somber than one might expect.

Noam pointed to Jesus and then to the disciples who walked behind him. "If that man were not riding a donkey—if he were walking among his followers—you would be hard-pressed to tell which of them was the master."

With a gleam in his eye, Jared pulled his brothers closer. "Consider what might be accomplished if these people were not *cheering* Jesus of Nazareth, but *following* him—or someone like him—in an uprising against Pilate and all those who conspire with him."

As the procession went past, Noam pointed to one of the dozen or so men trailing Jesus. "Isn't that Simon, our companion from our days in Galilee? Even now he follows the prophet from Nazareth."

Jared recognized the unmistakable gait of the man they had once known well. He waved for his brothers to follow and hurried to join the men leading the procession on the East Gate Road. Their unexpected and rapid approach startled the disciples, who responded defensively. One instinctively reached for what Jared presumed was a weapon.

The brothers stopped in their tracks, and Simon eased the tension by stepping forward to greet them. "Do not worry," he called over his shoulder to his fellow disciples. "Tell Peter to stand down. These men are my former associates. I believe they mean no harm." He stared directly at Jared and asked, "You *don't* mean any harm, do you?"

Jared put his arm around the disciple's shoulder and re-plied, "Simon, my dear friend, far be it from us to do harm to your teacher. You and we have always been of one mind."

"At one time we were of one mind," Simon corrected. "But now that I . . ."

The cheering and crowd noise prevented futher conver-sation. As Jesus and his disciples made their way through the city, the people who lined the streets fell in behind them. The procession continued to the temple, where Jesus dismounted.

The area outside the temple complex was packed with pilgrims and citizens bringing their offerings for sacrifices. The disciples, joined by Jared and his brothers, pushed past several people to stay close to Jesus.

The group entered the temple complex through the east gate. The walls of the complex extended hundreds of feet on either side of the gate. Once inside, the men climbed large stone steps that led to a small porch area. Two large white pillars stood at the front of the porch. At the back stood two elaborately carved doors that led to the main courtyard of the temple complex.

Jesus—and those who followed him—walked quickly to one of the two interior staircases that led up to the Court of Gentiles. They passed the balustrade with its signs that warned anyone who was not a Jewish male to proceed no farther, upon penalty of death.

In the outer courtyard of the temple, Jesus stopped. Merchants who sold cows and other animals for sacrifice sat at tables throughout the courtyard. Moneychangers who exchanged currency brought by foreign visitors for local currency—and who carved out a tidy profit for themselves in the process—were there, too, conducting their business in full view of the temple.

With a suddenness that startled Jared and several other onlookers, Jesus grabbed the table of a nearby merchant and hurled it over. He did the same with a moneychanger's table, sending coins flying in every direction.

In a voice that carried across the courtyard, he said, "It is written, 'My house shall be called a house of prayer,' but you make it a den of robbers."

Merchants scrambled to grab the money from their tables before the teacher from Nazareth turned his wrath on them. No one made a move to stop Jesus. The merchants and moneychangers tripped over one another trying to avoid him. Worshipers stared in disbelief. Temple officials retreated to the edges of the courtyard.

In the midst of the commotion, Jared pulled Simon aside. "Your teacher is filled with a passion for the temple. Might that passion be turned against the Roman rulers who defile our land with their presence?"

Simon didn't appear surprised by this daring—and dangerous—challenge to the establishment, but he quickly countered, "What about our own religious leaders who act like disobedient children? The teacher has repeatedly challenged them to change their ways and return to God, but to what end?"

Jared tried to hide his disdain, but his facial expression gave him away. Simon continued, "I believe we share a similar passion for righteousness, my friend, but we no longer agree as to how change must be accomplished."

Jared barked, "Change? Has anything changed since you've been following your feeble leader? Look around! Don't you see that we are still surrounded by Gentiles who defile us with their very presence? I want to see results—as you once did!"

He turned to leave, but Simon's hand on his shoulder stopped him. "If you really hope to understand our teacher's methods and his plan for change, you need to follow him and see for yourself."

Chapter 3

The Women
Jesus Knew

THE ROLE OF WOMEN IN 1ST CENTURY AD

Generally speaking, the world Jesus knew had changed from a patriarchal tradition in which women were considered the property of men with no rights to a society where Jewish women could acquire wealth and education. First-century Jews lived within a Hellenistic society. Women were beginning to have a voice in political and business matters. Most Jewish families trended toward Greek ways and ideas, and women found new roles and freedom.

By contrast, women in first-century China found themselves steeped in a patriarchal society that allowed concubinage. At marriage a woman moved from her family to the family of her new husband. Her standing within the marriage depended greatly on her ability to produce male heirs. Yet, even if a wife bore sons, her standing could be in jeopardy. Not until a wife became a grandmother did she have a similar position as her husband within the family structure.

In the Mayan culture, females were more central to the society. They worked in agricultural and textile industries, held positions as rulers in their cities, and served as priestesses at various sacred sites. While most filled traditional roles of caring for the household, many chose different lives.

In the Roman Empire, women were not regarded as equal to men before the law. They received only a basic education and were subject to the authority of a man—their father until they married, then their husband. First-century Roman women did enjoy certain freedoms, however, based on wealth and social status. A woman could own, inherit, and sell property. Even so, women could not vote.

In many ways, the position of Jewish women in first-century Israel was better than in most societies. Since Judaism believes that both man and woman are created equal in the image of God, there existed an opportunity for women to be more than subservient to their husbands or fathers. With the importance of family in the Jewish home, a woman's life was honored and respected. Also, women were not excluded from the synagogue, although they were prohibited from participation in certain religious activities.

Jesus frequently demonstrated an inclusive attitude toward women. Women supported his ministry and traveled with the disciples. He counted Mary and Martha, the sisters of Lazarus, among his closest friends. In the New Testament account of Jesus's resurrection, Mary Magdalene is given the honor of being the first witness to encounter the risen Jesus.

Dawn had already announced itself on the eastern horizon when Chana stirred and opened her eyes. Suspended between sleep and wakefulness, she struggled to make sense of her dimly lit surroundings. She wasn't in her own house; that much was certain. The unfamiliar sounds and smells that drifted through the window suggested that she wasn't even in Gennesaret.

A voice she recognized finally snapped her back to reality, for better or worse. It was the voice of her sister-in-law, singing softly as she prepared the morning meal in the courtyard. Chana glanced around the guest room in her brother's house and wondered if she would ever get used to it—or to the city of Jerusalem, or to life as a widow.

She dressed quickly and hurried downstairs and out to the courtyard. Lila was grinding wheat grain into flour. She stopped singing long enough to greet Chana with a thin smile. The strain of preparing her house for Passover was evident. Chana scooped a measure of the ground flour into a bowl, added oil to it, and began kneading it into dough.

"Reuben will take the Passover garments to the fuller this morning," Lila said.

"Will he be able to carry the basket by himself?" Chana asked. "He is still a child."

"He is a young man," Lila corrected her. "He has the strength to carry the basket. Yet he has not made the journey to the fuller himself. I will need you to show him the way before you visit your cousin this morning." She was too absorbed in her breadmaking to see Chana wince.

"I will show him the way," Chana said, somehow managing to keep her voice from divulging the repugnance she felt toward her assigned task.

"Go now," Lila insisted, "before the lines for the fuller grow too long. I will finish preparing the meal."

Chana returned to the house and put on her headdress. The Passover clothing lay folded in a basket near the front door. Reuben, her young nephew, apparently was no more eager to be chaperoned by his aunt on his maiden voyage to the fuller than Chana was to accompany him. The boy tried to hurry out the door ahead of her, but the basket proved to be too uncooperative. He struggled mightily to get a good grip on it. By the time he did, Chana was by his side.

The city of Jerusalem started to come alive as Chana and Reuben made their way through its streets. Merchants and their servants carried wares to the marketplace to begin another day of selling. Small groups of priests and other men spoke to one another in low, serious tones as they walked toward the temple. A few women carried baskets similar to Chana's. Chana quickened her pace in order to stay ahead of them. Reuben had no choice but to quicken his as well.

Chana held her breath as she passed through the north gate of the city. Reuben did not, a fact that was evident by the sour expression on his face. The unmistakable stench of the fullers at work hung heavy in the air. In an open field just outside the city wall, several tubs containing mixtures of water, human and animal urine, and other substances were arranged in rows. The water for the tubs came from the nearby pool of Gihon. Urine had been collected from public urinals and small jars set around the city.

Under the watchful eye of the fuller, bare-legged boys—about Reuben's age—stood in the tubs, stamping on garments or beating them with a stick. Others applied fuller's earth to clothes that hung from ropes strung between wooden poles. The cleansing concoction absorbed oils and grease, whitening the garments; the stamping and beating removed stains and smells.

Chana watched as Reuben wrested an assurance from the man that the cleaning and whitening of the family's clothes would be finished by midday. Young Reuben negotiated as his father had taught him. He reminded Chana a lot of his father when he was a boy. His errand complete, Reuben walked quickly past Chana without a glance as he returned home. Though she could not keep step with the spry youngster, Chana also hurried back toward the city—and away from the awful odor—as quickly as she could.

"Did you see his entry into the city? Did you hear the people cheering and the children singing?"

Chana cast a discreet glance to her left. Two women, coming from the direction of the east gate, fell in step with her. One woman wore a pale yellow tunic. The other woman's tunic was crimson, just slightly darker than Chana's.

The woman in crimson laughed softly. "It seemed at the time that most of us in Jerusalem had gathered to lay palm branches before him and shout, 'Hosanna!'

"Our caravan was still a half-day's journey away when the news reached us," the woman in yellow explained. "One of the men who journeyed with us, a worker in the synagogue in Capernaum, called it blasphemy and said that the crowd of Galileans was stirred to a frenzy. Those of us in the caravan who follow Jesus said nothing. We just quietly lamented that we were not here to witness his entry."

"I have been told that the chief priests have begun to keep a watchful eye on him," the woman in crimson noted. "Yet I have not seen them try to hinder his coming and going."

Ahead of her, Chana saw several young men approaching. Each of them was carrying a lamb. The men did not slow their pace or even alter their course as they neared Chana. She had to step aside in order to let them pass. The women next to her did not and continued walking.

Chana caught up to the women near the table of a merchant who sold pottery, lamps, and baking dishes. All three women stopped to admire a cooking pot whose shape was new to them. The merchant turned briefly to look at the women but continued his pitch to a young man standing at the table. According to the merchant, the pot was a new style, recently created by Roman artisans.

The merchant glanced over his shoulder again. The women took the hint and started to walk away.

Chana could contain herself no longer. "Forgive me," she said quietly. She touched one of the women on the elbow. Both women turned to face her. The smiles they offered were so warm and inviting that she felt no self-consciousness about having interrupted their conversation. "Are you speaking of the teacher from Nazareth?"

The women's smiles grew wider. "We follow Jesus of Nazareth," the woman in yellow explained. "Do you know of him?"

She pointed to an area of shade beneath a nearby palm tree, and the three women made their way there.

Chana returned their smiles and introduced herself. She learned that the woman in crimson was named Phyllis and the woman in yellow was named Miriam.

"I know little about the teacher you follow," Chana admitted. "And what I do know I have been told by others. I come from Gennesaret. There I know a young woman who suffered for years from bleeding that would not stop."

"For years she was unclean," Phyllis noted.

Chana nodded. "She grew desperate. When she heard that Jesus would be passing through our town, she tried to see him."

"She joined the crowd in her state of uncleanness?" Miriam asked.

Chana felt a pang of shame and embarrassment on the woman's behalf. "As I said, she was desperate."

Miriam and Phyllis nodded their understanding.

Chana continued. "She told us later that she could not get close to your teacher because so many others had come to him for healing. She said the only thing she could do was to reach out and touch his cloak as he passed by."

"And what happened?" The twinkle in Miriam's eye suggested that she knew the answer to her own question.

Chana paused for a moment before she replied. "She said her bleeding stopped the moment she touched his cloak."

"Did you believe her?"

The directness of Miriam's question startled Chana. "I thought—that is, well, I *saw* that she no longer suffered from the bleeding."

"Did you wonder how that came to be?"

Chana took a deep breath and exhaled. "I do not wish to offend you or your teacher. This matter has not left my mind for more than a year now. I know what I saw when she returned to Gennesaret. I know what I heard when she told me the story. Yet I also know that physicians use herbs, ointments, and wraps to accomplish their healing. What I wonder is if either of you have seen your teacher heal in this manner."

Phyllis turned toward Miriam. Neither woman's smile faded.

"I was lying sick on a mat in my home in Capernaum," Miriam began. "I had a fever and could not move. Jesus entered my home and touched my hand."

"Your teacher entered your house?" Chana asked.

"My son-in-law Simon—the one Jesus calls Peter—is his disciple," Miriam explained.

"What happened when he touched your hand?"

"My fever left me *immediately*," Miriam said, perhaps more loudly than she intended. "My strength returned. I got up from my mat and ministered to my guests. With a single touch, he healed me of my sickness."

She and Chana were too engrossed in their conversation to notice the eavesdropper. Phyllis spotted him, though—and her face went white. She lowered her head and whispered for Miriam and Chana to do the same. Chana did as she was instructed, but not before stealing a quick glance.

A priest stood in the street near them, staring in their direction. He seemed to be weighing Miriam's words, perhaps wondering what to do about these women who spoke so openly about the controversial teacher from Nazareth.

Chana's heart beat wildly, uncertain about what was happening.

The priest considered them for a long moment before turning and walking quickly in the direction of the temple.

"Come with us!" Phyllis whispered to Chana. "Many of the priests are outraged about how the people are responding to Jesus. He might return, and we would rather not have to explain our comments. My house is not far from here." Chana did not need to be asked twice. Her cousin could wait another day for her visit. Neither she nor her companions spoke as they hurried through the streets of Jerusalem. Occasionally one of them would glance over her shoulder to make sure no one was following.

"Here it is!" Phyllis finally announced. Her small house sat nestled between two much larger homes. The three women rushed inside, passed through two brightly lit rooms, and stepped into the courtyard. Safely out of sight and earshot of potentially threatening strangers, they began to relax.

After some time, Chana turned to Phyllis. "Have you been healed by the teacher from Nazareth as well?"

Phyllis shook her head. In a voice barely louder than a whisper, she explained, "I have not asked him to heal me of any afflictions. But I have been a witness to his miracles. I have seen him restore sight to the blind and drive demons from the afflicted."

Chana could find no reply. She stared at Phyllis with her mouth open.

"Come with us to see him tomorrow," Miriam urged her.

"I have no afflictions to be healed," Chana countered.

"The *words* Jesus speaks are as powerful as his healing touch," Phyllis explained. "He teaches us to love our enemies and to bless those who curse us. He teaches us to forgive others like God forgives us."

"He speaks with an authority that other teachers do not have," Miriam added.

"I have no husband or son," Chana continued. Tears filled her eyes. "Will your teacher from Nazareth show me compassion?"

"Yes!" came the simultaneous reply.

"You will not be turned away," Phyllis continued. "His kindness extends to women. He is affirming and welcoming to *all* people."

Chana looked at Phyllis and then at Miriam. "You both speak of your teacher's kindness. You speak of his healing. You speak of his friendship. Yet you say nothing of what he demands in return. What does Jesus ask of those who follow him?"

Miriam offered Chana her warmest smile yet.

"Come and see."

Chapter 4

The Travel
Jesus Knew

TRAVEL AND TRANSPORTATION
IN 1ST CENTURY AD

The people who lived in the world Jesus knew were beneficiaries of remarkable advances in travel and transportation. In China, many of the key advances involved water travel and trade. Beginning in the second century BC, a great trade route originating from Chang'an (now Xian) took shape to link China with the Roman world. This route circulated precious goods and opened cultural exchanges between China, India, Persia, Greece, and Rome.

The land-based counterpart to China's Silk Road was the network of roads that connected the Roman Empire. Built by legions of Roman soldiers, not to mention an untold number of slaves and prisoners of war, the Roman road system was a marvel of technology and labor.

To build a Roman road, a trench was dug four to five feet deep. The bottom of the trench was pounded solid. In some places, supports were driven to shore up unsteady ground. A foot-deep layer of masonry, set in cement or clay, served as the base. Successive layers of concrete, gravel, and cement—each more than a foot thick—were laid over the base. The surface was dressed stone, carefully sloped from the center to promote drainage. The average Roman road was about ten yards wide, enough to accommodate two full-size wagons abreast.

At its peak, the Roman network of roads covered more than 50,000 miles. Posthouses, stocked with fresh horses, were set up every ten miles along the way to accommodate the quick relay of information throughout the empire. Inns and lodging houses could be found every twenty miles or so. The roads were heavily patrolled by the Roman military, and watchtowers were built at specific intervals to ensure travelers' safety.

Even so, pilgrimage to the temple was a demanding challenge for foreign Jewish worshipers. Nazareth to Jerusalem was at least seventy to seventy-five miles by foot and donkey. It would have taken nearly four days at a maximum of twenty miles per day. The journey was dangerous and hard, particularly difficult for the elderly and children. Locals from Galilee were fortunate to make it to Jerusalem once a year. Pilgrimages from the east of Egypt or North Africa were most likely a rare event—perhaps once in a lifetime.

E li studied the faces of the people who had gathered and were waiting to accompany their teacher on the short journey from Bethany to Jerusalem. He wondered how many of them could sense that something was amiss. Had any of them considered that this trip might be Jesus's last? How many had the slightest inkling that the end of this crowd-pleasing three-year odyssey was in sight?

Jesus sensed it; Eli was certain of that. A rumor making its way through the crowd suggested that Jesus had discussed his upcoming death with his disciples more than once in recent days. Perhaps he was finally starting to recognize—too late—the dangers of making powerful enemies.

Most of those who gathered that morning seemed oblivious to the dark clouds on the horizon. They expected the journey from Bethany to proceed as their previous travels with Jesus had. Jesus would lead the way and he didn't seem to be on any particular schedule.

Sometimes Jesus of Nazareth might speak to those around him; sometimes he might remain quiet for the better part of a day, lost in thought about something he chose not to share. Sometimes he would walk as a man with a purpose, eager to reach his destination. Other times, his destination would seem to be of secondary concern to him. He would point out sights along the way—a mustard seed, a flock of sheep, a fishing net—and build a parable from them.

Eli chuckled softly to himself as he thought of the way most people responded to Jesus's parables. The Nazarene inevitably triggered confused glances among his audience—from the conservative Galileans to the more diverse Judeans.

They all struggled to comprehend the meaning in the stories he told.

Much of the time they missed the whole point. Eli recalled embarking on a journey of several days as part of an earlier covert assignment to discover more about Jesus of Nazareth. He was with a group who spent one night at a typical inn, the kind that could be found at twenty-mile intervals along most Roman roads. The two-storied structure was built around a large central courtyard. Travelers slept side by side on the floor of the second story, with only exterior walls and archways protecting them from the elements. Their animals were housed in stalls below them on the ground floor.

The inn was particularly crowded that night. The men in Jesus's entourage were forced to sleep shoulder to shoulder, with very little room between their sleeping mats. The crowded conditions made it easy to listen to other people's conversations. That's how Eli overheard two of Jesus's disciples marveling over the fact that Jesus had started his life in just such an inn in the town of Bethlehem. The only difference was, he had not been born on the second floor; he had been born on the ground, among the animals, because the second floor had been too crowded for his parents to find room.

While the rest of the group was busy celebrating Jesus's humble origins among the animals and feeding troughs, they failed to recognize that—if the story were true—his origins weren't nearly as humble as they believed. If Jesus had, in fact, been born in an inn in Bethlehem, then he was not Galilean at all. The little town of Bethlehem lay squarely in Judea.

Eli heard shuffling and saw that the assembled group was finally beginning to move toward Jerusalem. He elbowed the man standing to his left, a man he had identified as a fellow Judean from his earliest days of following Jesus. Gesturing toward Jesus, Eli said, "Now he must return to the temple and answer to the priests for the chaos and disruption he caused there."

The man on his left started to reply, but had no opportunity to do so. Before he could speak, a man on Eli's right responded loudly and forcefully enough for everyone in the general vicinity to hear.

"Jesus will answer to no one!" He seemed genuinely impressed at Jesus' power and grit, certainly rare among synagogue teachers.

Eli sighed, but refused to turn his head. He would not give the man the satisfaction.

Another man shouted, "The Judeans have created a temple where righteous men will not set foot!" the man yelled, even though Eli was standing right next to him. "How can those who bargain with our Roman overlords also speak for the God of Israel? And still you demand Galilean tithes and taxes for your perverse ways."

"Those who daily attend to the temple might say the Galileans are lax in their observance of Jewish customs," Eli replied. "The road from Galilee runs straight and true. It is not a long journey. Yet Galileans cannot be bothered to enter Solomon's Porch, let alone to enter the holy temple, which is their sacred duty."

Eli seized the opening. He turned to face his opponent for the first time. "Do you object?"

The man seemed to sense that he was being led into trap of logic. "It is the responsibility of every righteous man to object to pagan rulers," he replied carefully.

"That's why righteous men rid themselves of denarii, the coins of Rome, which are stamped with the images of pagan rulers." He couldn't help himself from emphasizing the last two words.

"The sacred duty of the moneychangers in the temple," Eli continued, "is to exchange the foreign coins of pagans for the shekels that are acceptable to the God of Israel. Yet the moneychangers were the very people Jesus chose to attack in the temple. That is why I said he would have something to answer for today. All his angry disturbance accomplished was to make it more difficult for righteous people to fulfill their duties to the Lord." Eli knew he probably should have stopped there, but such ideal opportunities for gloating rarely presented themselves. "If you Galileans left your northern district more often for Jerusalem, you might understand such things."

"Empty your coin pouch." Eli heard the command coming from behind him.

He turned and found himself face-to-face with the disciple Jesus called "Peter." The burly, bearded disciple was staring hard at him. "Empty your coin pouch," he repeated.

Eli felt his face flush. He tried to speak, but his words skittered away from him before they could be voiced. "I—" was all he could manage.

"If Roman coins so offend you, you surely will not be in possession of even one denarius because it is engraved with the image of Caesar," he continued. "Let us take measure of the faithful observance of a Judean. Open your coin pouch."

The man with whom Eli had debated smiled—pleased, no doubt, to have such a powerful ally speak for him. Sensing a confrontation, others gathered around the three men. Eli cast a glance in Jesus's direction, afraid that he, too, would join the conversation. He was relieved to see the teacher far out of earshot, talking with some children.

Eli considered his options. It was one thing to debate a Galilean follower on the outskirts of the crowd, but to tangle publicly with one of Jesus's primary disciples might prove to be a tactical error. He chose to bide his time.

Eli offered the imposing fisherman an abashed smile. "I will not open my coin pouch." His voice was the very essence of contriteness. "It is not for fear that you will find a Roman coin, but rather that you will discover that I have not given everything, as did the widow whom I understand the teacher praises so lavishly."

Simon Peter considered his answer for a moment but then walked away without saying another word. Eli watched him go and thought to himself, *This isn't over.*

The short journey from Bethany proceeded as most journeys with Jesus did, with the disciples jockeying for position near the teacher. Simon Peter walked, as he almost always did, on Jesus's right side. Ten other disciples filled in the spaces to his left and behind him. The twelfth lagged behind as the caravan approached Jerusalem, content to take up a position near the back. Eli lingered with him.

"You argue as one whose father changes money in the temple," Judas Iscariot said after they had walked some distance. His words likely were a joke at Eli's expense. (Eli couldn't tell from the man's expressionless demeanor.) Yet in them, Eli saw an opening.

"Shall it always be thus," he asked the disciple, "that those who manage money will be accused of villainy and wrongdoing?" He had to suppress a smile when he saw Judas's body stiffen. His words had found their mark.

"What shall I say to you in this matter?" Eli continued. "You know better than most what it is to collect and disburse money. You were tasked with the responsibility by the teacher himself."

"Yes," Judas acknowledged with a shrug and a sly smile, "because the only other candidates were fishermen and a tax collector."

"Yet you have proven yourself wise in the ways of money," Eli countered. "I saw you in the home of the leper when that foolish woman poured perfume over the teacher's feet. Everyone else in the house marveled at her faithfulness. Even the teacher commended her. Yet only you saw the true expense of her actions. I could see it in your face and in the way you left the house in distress. You alone recognized what might have been accomplished if the woman had sold the perfume and given you the money instead."

"Your words tell me I was not alone in my understanding of such things," Judas said.

"Yet is your wisdom rewarded?" Eli pressed. "Do the others appreciate the personal sacrifices and expenses that the keeper of the money incurs? I have found that treasurers, like moneychangers, are often subjected to the cruelest accusations and gossip."

"Every coin that cannot be accounted for is a cause for investigation," Judas muttered.

Eli cleared his throat, giving himself an extra moment to decide whether to proceed. He chose his next words carefully. "There are others—important people in Jerusalem—who have recognized your skills . . . and your unique position."

There it was—everything almost said.

Judas seemed to grasp Eli's meaning immediately. He was so quick to grasp it, in fact, that Eli wondered if the disciple had been warned about such entreaties or coached on how to recognize them.

A roar in the distance interrupted the disciple's reply. A large crowd had gathered at Jerusalem's east gate to await Jesus's arrival. Eli turned to Judas to remark on the crowd's size, but the disciple was already making his way to the front of the group. Eli watched him weave through the throng of followers to rejoin his fellow disciples. He held his breath for a moment when Judas stopped to talk to Simon Peter. The fisherman did not turn to look in Eli's direction, which likely meant that Judas had said nothing about their conversation, which likely meant . . .

Eli smiled.

As the crowd at the gate swarmed the caravan from Bethany, Eli lost sight of Judas. Thanks to a few propitious surges and jostlings in the crowd, however, he found himself very near Jesus and Simon Peter as they entered the city and made their way to the temple.

Eli saw that three women had taken a position between the teacher from Nazareth and his close disciple. Eli judged the women to be widows, since they were not accompanied by husbands.

The older woman nearest Simon Peter wore a pale yellow cloak. When she stumbled slightly over a palm branch, he reached out to steady her with a son's concern and affection. She repaid his gesture with a loving pat on the cheek. The other two women—another older woman and a young one—wore red cloaks. The young woman nearest Jesus trembled in his presence, as though she was encountering him for the first time. Despite the pandemonium erupting all around him, the teacher from Nazareth did not look away from the woman.

Eli shook his head again. It was beyond his comprehension why many of his fellow priests were so rattled by this man who welcomed widows, lepers, and the demon-possessed. His blasphemy would be enough to condemn him, but beyond that, he certainly posed no threat.

Several of the priests were waiting outside the temple when Jesus arrived. The crowd pressed forward on all sides, eager to see a showdown. The atmosphere was not hostile, but it was tense, so a couple of the disciples escorted the women away. Some of the priests wanted explanations for Jesus's prior actions regarding the moneychangers in the temple, but he offered no response. At that point Peter walked up and stood beside Jesus, together facing the priests. When neither side offered further provocation, the priests returned to the temple and the crowd began to disperse.

A spark of anger ignited in Eli's chest against Peter. He still tasted the words he had swallowed—for the greater good—after their previous altercation. They were bitter in his throat.

The indignity of being challenged by a net-minder, one whose skin reeked of fish, ate at him. How could he be expected to respond to a language that barely qualified as Aramaic? Were there no schools at all in Galilee? How else could one explain the dropped consonants, the lazy speech patterns, and the thick accent that garbled even the wisest utterances?

Eli vowed that he would take his revenge on the disciple—in full view of an audience—as soon as his mission had been accomplished. So intense was Eli's focus on Peter that he almost didn't notice Judas sidling up next to him.

The time for innuendo and coy advances was over, Eli decided in that moment. He nodded toward Jesus. "Your teacher challenges the priests and drives out the moneychangers. Yet he accomplishes nothing. The priests remain and the moneychangers return."

Eli waved his hand toward the crowded temple entrance. "Every day multitudes come here with their offerings and sacrifices. When your teacher is dead, multitudes more will continue to come with their offerings and sacrifices. He will have changed nothing, and you will have nothing to show for your years of service."

Judas stared into the distance.

"For years now, your teacher has challenged long-respected views of the priests and teachers of the Law. Yet what has your opposition accomplished? Has Jesus broken the backs of the chief priests and scribes? Has their power been given to him?

"And what have you gained for your troubles? Are you wealthier than you were three years ago? Are you more celebrated? Are you more respected? I am here to tell you that the men you may believe to be enemies can be your benefactors."

Judas nodded once and then dropped his chin to his chest, as though the weight of his head were too much for his neck to bear. In a voice barely loud enough for Eli to hear, the disciple asked a single question:

"What would you have me do?"

Chapter 5

The Economy Jesus Knew

TRADE AND COMMERCE IN 1ST CENTURY AD

Trade and commerce in the first century AD was spurred by opportunity and need. Through careful cultivation and management of land, labor, and resources, many Roman provinces established a surplus of agricultural goods. These surpluses made the provinces attractive trade partners with other provinces and other nations. The goods exchanged in these trades included food and drink (olives, fish, meat, cereals, wine, beer), manufacturing materials (glass, marble, wood, bricks, gold, silver, copper, tin), animal products (leather and hides), and pottery. Human slaves also figured prominently in the trade markets of Jesus's day.

Despite Rome's ever-expanding network of well-built roads, merchants overwhelmingly preferred to transport their goods by sea. Water travel was so much cheaper and faster that it was worth the constant risks of pirates and storms. Numerous ports on the Red Sea and Mediterranean accommodated a growing number of trading partners for Roman and Palestinian merchants and manufacturers.

As the empire and its economy grew, so did its need for imported goods. Feeding the massive Roman army was an enormous undertaking in itself. Fortunately, Rome's trade partners were equal to the task. Archaeologists have discovered the remains of large estates in France that were capable of storing 100,000 liters of wine, olive presses in Libya that were capable of producing 100,000 liters of olive oil per year, and gold mines in Spain that yielded more than 9,000 kilograms of gold per year.

Other merchants from Rome, Egypt, and Palestine trafficked in exotic goods from Arabia, India, and even China. These goods included pepper, cloves, ginger, cinnamon, colored marble, silk, perfumes, and ivory.

For Roman officials to control trade throughout the empire, the state established a merchant fleet of its own. A typical vessel in the fleet could transport roughly 75 tons of goods, though some larger ships could transport well over 300 tons.

One official was appointed to oversee each area of trade. For example, the official in charge of grain was expected to regulate the various ship owners who trafficked in grain to maintain a steady flow. By taxing the transportation of goods between provinces and issuing permits for local markets, the state could keep its thumb on—and benefit financially from—commerce at all levels.

The state also worked to control trade and prevent fraud by stamping goods such as pottery, bricks, glass, wooden barrels, and the metal ingots (molds) used to make coins with marks that identified their manufacturers or guaranteed their weight or purity. In some cases, the marks also identified the merchants who transported the goods and the officials who oversaw the process. Yet Rome's tentacles could only extend so far. Historians have discovered evidence of a thriving free-market economy that operated beyond the reach of the empire.

The enormity of Rome's economy and consumption of goods—more than twenty-three million kilograms of oil and two million hectoliters of wine annually—would not be seen again until the Industrial Revolution.

The Jewish people debated whether or not they should contribute to the occupying Romans. Rome demanded exorbitant taxes, seventy percent of which went directly to the Roman military. The Israelites bitterly resented the taxation—in many cases, they had to do without necessities to afford the payments—but they were forced to give what was demanded. Most could see no other option than to participate in Roman commerce and support the Roman economy.

In addition, Rome capitalized on the major Jewish feast days. Roman officials, not to mention the Jewish aristocracy who aided and abetted them, found ways to turn pilgrimages into revenue streams. From the inns where travelers stayed on their long journeys, to the food and souvenirs they purchased during their stay in Jerusalem, to the animals they bought for sacrifices and offerings in the temple, large crowds of Jewish pilgrims contributed mightily to the coffers of Rome.

The merchant and governing classes of Rome were wealthy, lived in the best villas, ate the finest food, and dressed in magnificent clothes. Life was luxurious, extravagant, and indulgent. The same was true for the Herodian leaders in Jerusalem. They held privilege, much of which came from heavy taxation. It's little wonder that some Jewish dissidents targeted instruments of Roman commerce and trade in their rebellions.

Jared tracked Jesus's approach by the sounds of his entourage getting louder. The small roar that went up from the east gate of the city grew steadily as more and more people joined the group on the way to the temple. Jared and his companions were not the only ones awaiting his arrival.

"The vultures are perched and ready to feast," Jared's older brother Noam noted. He nodded to the handful of priests and elders who had gathered in the outer court of the temple. They appeared to be monitoring the approach of the popular teacher from Nazareth as well.

"He made himself their prey when he attacked their corrupt system," his younger brother Seth replied. "They have come to put the Galilean in his place."

Uri, the elderly man who had opened his home to the brothers, shook his head. "No vulture was ever so apprehensive about its prey. Look at the way their eyes shift, the way they lick their dry lips. These men did not come to challenge Jesus of Nazareth by their own choice. They were sent by others too wise and too cautious to confront him themselves."

"I wish the teacher would use his reasoned arguments to convince his followers to challenge Rome," Jared suggested.

Jesus arrived at the temple court before Uri or Jared's brothers could reply. The man was no one's idea of what a prophet would look like. Jared's mood of hopeful anticipation quickly changed to annoyed disappointment.

Yet his annoyance paled in comparison to that of the gathered priests and elders. These men were accustomed to receiving respectful nods and reverent greetings in the temple. Jesus was so engrossed in conversation with his followers and the larger, curious crowds that he walked past the assembled priests without even acknowledging their presence. The outraged leaders gestured and whispered to one another as they trailed Jesus's group to Solomon's Porch.

Under the roof of the white colonnade, Jesus turned to face his followers, who scrambled to find seats at his feet. He also noticed the religious leaders lingering nearby and paused. He stared at them for a moment and gestured ever-so-subtly to the crowd. From where Chana stood, it appeared that he was inviting them to say whatever was on their minds.

"By what authority are you doing these things, and who gave you this authority?" one the priests interrupted loudly enough for people in the outer court to hear. A silence fell over the group, punctured only by a few gasps and a single cough. Passersby became bystanders as they stopped to watch the burgeoning confrontation. All eyes turned to Jesus.

"I also will ask you one question," Jesus replied, "and if you tell me the answer, then I also will tell you by what authority I do these things." The crowd murmured, and the priests shifted uncomfortably where they stood.

"The baptism of John," Jesus continued, "from where did it come? From heaven or from man?"

Uri smiled as he watched the priests and elders huddled. "Once again they underestimate the man's wisdom," he told his young friends.

"Why does he speak of the Baptizer in this matter?" Seth asked.

"He has given the priests a choice they cannot make," Uri explained. "John was a popular prophet who attracted large crowds. If the priests say his power came from men, then the people will rise up against them. If they say his power came from heaven, then the Nazarene will ask why they opposed him. He has left them with only two options: either they will admit their ignorance or they will storm off in a fit of anger."

"We do not know," one of the priests admitted a moment later.

"Neither will I tell you by what authority I do these things," Jesus replied.

The priests and elders traipsed away, stopping only for a moment to glare at the old man with white hair and three young men who seemed to be greatly amused.

Jesus turned his attention back to his followers. "What do you think?" he began. "A man had two sons—"

Jared motioned for his brothers to follow him. The three managed to slip away from Jesus's entourage without drawing undue attention to themselves. Uri watched them go. He gave them a quick wave as they headed elsewhere in the temple.

In the Court of the Gentiles, the business of the temple was booming. Tables filled with caged doves, oils, wines, and the coins of moneychangers littered the area. Every year the selections seemed to increase as merchants had discovered Jerusalem to be a lucrative location to market their wares—especially during the Jewish festivals and holy ceremonies.

"Are there not one hundred more vendors now than there were the last time we entered this temple?" Noam asked.

"Every coin these vendors collect is split with their Roman overseers." Jared spoke loud enough for the vendor nearest him to hear. The man turned, looked the brothers up and down, and muttered something about "Galileans." Before the final syllable left his lips, Seth sent him sprawling with a hard shoulder to his back. The man tumbled headfirst over his table as hundreds of coins from Tyre and dozens of foreign lands clattered to the ground.

A crowd gathered to help the man, who lay on his left side with the table on top of him. He tried to direct people's attention to Seth, but the breath had been knocked from his lungs and his right arm was injured. All he could do was moan and tilt his head in Seth's direction. The three brothers disappeared into the crowd without a backward glance.

They hurried through the chest-high balustrade that separated the Court of the Gentiles from the temple proper. At each gate of the balustrade, a sign warned foreigners and Gentiles to proceed no farther. Past the balustrade, they climbed fourteen steps and crossed the short terrace to a second set of stairs that ascended to an inner wall.

Beyond the wall, they passed through the gold- and silver-plated eastern gate of the Court of Women. Several women lined the courtyard, but they were careful to keep clear the path that led to the western end of the court.

Jared and his brothers made their way to the semicircular staircase that took them up to the Court of the Israelites—the farthest they could go in the temple. The long, narrow courtyard was uncomfortably full. A line of men waited near the square-cut stones that separated the Court of the Israelites from the Court of the Priests. Some of the men held caged doves; others held wineskins and jugs of oil.

A priest walked a lamb past the line of men and up the short staircase that led to the massive altar where sacrifices were made.

A man at the back of the line, who was holding a caged dove, muttered, "Long live the emperor," in a voice that suggested he wished anything but a long life for the emperor of Rome.

'Why do you speak such words in this place?" Seth demanded.

Nodding toward the priest with the lamb, the man explained, "That was Eliab. Every day he makes an offering for Caesar."

Seth gave his brothers a confused look and then turned back toward the man. "A *temple priest*," he said slowly, "makes an offering every day for the emperor who causes our people to starve while he demands taxes from us? A *priest of Israel* seeks God's blessing every day for the Roman leader who oppresses our nation with his greed? A *priest of God* defiles the altar of this temple every day with the blood of an animal sacrificed for a pagan?"

"Yes," the man told him. "He prospers greatly from it. Eliab's house is one of the largest in the city."

Seth's incredulity was quickly approaching rage. Jared noticed his younger brother's hand had slipped inside his cloak. He and Noam exchanged a quick glance, both clearly aware of what he was thinking. Jared placed his hand on Seth's shoulder; Noam took him by the elbow. "Let us carefully consider our next move," Jared whispered to him.

Seth tensed just for a moment as his brothers tried to lead him away. He made a slight move toward the stairs.

Jared and Noam tightened their grips. "If we are to give our lives for something, let it be for something grand—something that will be remembered long after we're gone," Noam urged him.

Seth relaxed as his brothers led him away.

As they walked, an idea occurred to Jared, one that he struggled to put into words. "We need independence from this corruption that plagues our people who are trying to follow the Torah," he said. He paused, and his eyes narrowed. He pulled his brothers close and asked, "Did you see the teacher from Nazareth? Those priests and elders crawled away from him like whimpering dogs. And that's how every man who witnessed their humiliation will see them from now on—every time they come to the temple, every time they pass them in the street, every time someone mentions their names. The sword and dagger can kill only once, but such embarrassment can wound again and again."

"You are suggesting that we throw our lot in with the teacher from Nazareth?" Noam asked. "True, he is a gifted orator who can put disgraceful priests in their place, but our people have placed their hopes in other so-called messiahs who came and went and no one now remembers. Besides, I for one don't think we share his message."

"Still," Jared replied, "he opposes the men we oppose, and he does so fearlessly. From such fertile common ground, alliances are grown. For now, he can be useful to us."

"He opposes *some* of the men we oppose," corrected Seth, with a poorly controlled tone of anger in his voice. "It's one thing for him to scold temple priests. But I don't hear him speaking up against the real problem—the Romans." Noam and Jared conceded the point with silence.

As they approached Solomon's Porch again, Jared was relieved to discover that the moneychanger Seth injured had been taken away. Jared could see Jesus, half-hidden behind a column, gesturing broadly to his audience. Uri stood nearby, with his back to Jesus and his followers, talking with three men. Neither he nor his companions seemed to be listening to the firebrand prophet speaking in metaphoric stories next to them.

Uri spotted Jared and his brothers while they were still some distance away. He spoke a few final words to the men around him and then stepped forward to greet his young houseguests. His companions scattered in three different directions before Jared could get a good look at them.

"Have you paid your temple tax yet?" Uri asked with a crooked smile.

Seth started to answer him—loudly—until the old man held up his index finger and then motioned for them to step closer.

"I just received news of a tax collector badly beaten, along with a merchant in the marketplace who was known to spy on other merchants for Pilate."

The brothers' eyes danced with excitement.

"There is also news that a small Roman supply caravan was attacked outside the city." The old man paused long enough to smile again. "Roman officials do not suspect highwaymen of the attack because the supplies were not stolen. They were burned."

Jared was trying to figure how Uri would have heard of such things. He asked, "Those men you were just speaking with . . . Who . . . ?"

Uri's eyes immediately signaled caution. He looked around, as nonchalantly as possible, and lowered his voice. "Hold your questions, my young friends. They shall all be answered soon enough."

"Shall we add to those victories by visiting the home of Eliab tonight?" Seth urged. Hoping his older brothers might reconsider, he pulled his cloak open to reveal his dagger.

Uri gave him an emphatic headshake. "*Nothing* will be done to the temple priests before the days of Passover are completed. More people than can be counted have descended on this city to celebrate and offer sacrifices. Any group that interferes with that—no matter how righteous their cause may be—won't have to worry about Rome. They will face the wrath of the people of Israel."

Seth closed his cloak and hung his head. Uri placed a hand on his shoulder and again lowered his voice. "Passion for what you believe in is a good thing, but such passion must be properly channeled if you want it to be effective."

Jared nodded toward the group that was still sitting in rapt attention, hanging on every word Jesus spoke. "We have discussed throwing our lot in with this man," he explained to Uri. "He strikes fear into the hearts of priests and elders now. In time, his approach may be best to subdue the corrupt Jewish leaders . . . and maybe even Roman rule!"

"Your reasoning is sound, but your judgment is flawed," Uri replied. "The teacher from Nazareth has no political ambition. Our common friend Simon knows this better than anyone. According to him, every time an opportunity presents itself to gather a small army of enthusiastic followers, Jesus retreats." He pointed to the crowd at Jesus's feet. "He commands a legion of followers much larger than this, yet he gives them no marching orders. He seeks no audience with Caesar, Pilate, or even the high priest."

Uri's words had the ring of finality, yet Jared could see a spark in the old man's eyes that suggested possibilities Jared couldn't fathom. He threw up his arms in frustration.

Uri flashed a smile that affirmed he knew more than he was saying. "The fact that this teacher from Nazareth will not lead his followers into battle does not mean they can't be led into battle. If they will not fight to *obey* him, then perhaps they will fight to *avenge* him."

Noam and Seth stared blankly at the man. Jared nodded slowly as the meaning of his words became clear.

Uri took a few steps backward and pointed discreetly toward the group. "Notice the one who stands behind him and never leaves his side." Jared and his brothers stepped forward and saw a powerfully built man with a dark beard. His head swiveled slowly back and forth, as he searched for threats and enemies in the crowd.

"Even in the safety of the temple, he has reached for his sword at least six times since his teacher started speaking," Uri said. "What might he do if a real danger presented itself?"

The three brothers studied the man for a moment.

"Does he know how to use the sword?" Seth asked.

"Will others follow him?" Noam asked.

"When will a real danger present itself?" Jared asked. That was the question Uri chose to answer.

"A servant of the high priest has told us that Caiaphas plans to arrest the teacher from Nazareth before the Passover week ends."

Chapter 6

The Religions Jesus Knew

RELIGIONS AND BELIEF SYSTEMS
IN 1ST CENTURY AD

With the exception of Islam, which would not be founded for another five centuries, many of the world's major religions had been firmly established by the first century AD. In China, the rulers of the Han Dynasty were urged to incorporate into their government the tenets of what Western scholars later termed "Confucianism." This humanist belief system held that the world existed in a harmonious state, in which various people's roles and influences worked together to create a greater good. The role of the ruler was to educate the people, to lead by moral example, and to make decisions to ensure the happiness and prosperity of his people. By the first century, Han rulers had incorporated the worship of ancestors and various deities into this belief system.

The seeds of Buddhism had been sown in India four centuries before the birth of Jesus. Siddhartha Gautama, a wandering ascetic and critic of the ancient Vedic religion of India, lived during the fifth century BC. After his death, his followers used his teachings to build a belief system that focused on the connection between desire and suffering and introduced an "eightfold path" for eliminating desire. During Jesus's lifetime, a new school of Buddhism emerged in northern India. The Mahayana school encouraged adaptability and innovation and is today the dominant form of Buddhism in China, Japan, Korea, Vietnam, Mongolia, Tibet, and Nepal.

Judaism had been the dominant belief system of the people of Israel well before 333 BC when Alexander the Great's conquests established the Greek Empire. The Abrahamic covenant had been the core of Judaism prior to Alexander, yet inhabitants of Palestine also worshiped other gods and performed rites of various other religions.

The Tanakh—the Hebrew Bible consisting of the Torah, Neviim, and Ketuvim (Instruction, Prophets, and Writings)—is the sacred text of Judaism, in conjunction with the Talmud and Midrash, which are rabbinic and legal interpretations of the Torah. Worship centered first in the tabernacle, then the temple, and after the destruction of the Second Temple, in synagogues. The temple had specific functions for sacrifice while the synagogue was a place of community gathering.

By the first century AD, numerous interpretations had been proposed for how best to fulfill and advance the Torah, and there was much discussion and dispute between various sects and schools of thought about which view was the correct one.

Outside of leaders and teachers, Jews tended to follow what their parents taught them, creating a simple piety among the people.

Many teachers, including Jesus, taught that the basic truths of the Torah could be summed up in two essential elements: (1) Love God with all your heart, mind, soul, and strength; and (2) Love your neighbor as yourself.

A heady swirl of emotions threatened to overwhelm Chana as she followed Jesus's entourage into the temple. Her legs trembled. She stayed close to the wall and used it to steady herself as she tried to keep pace with men much younger than she was. Her heart raced, partially due to the exertion but primarily due to the fact that Jesus had given her his full attention.

He had smiled when Phyllis introduced her at the east gate of the city. He had looked into her eyes. He had spoken gently to her, like a son to his mother. He had called her by name.

Hundreds of people had clamored for his attention as he made his way to the temple. They yelled his name. They waved palm branches in his direction. They stepped into the street in front of him. When he ignored those distractions, many took a different approach and began yelling at Chana for wasting the teacher's time.

Not once did any of them interrupt Jesus's conversation with her.

He spoke of many things on that walk, telling stories of watchful brides, perseverance through hardships, and how servants need to be wise about what is entrusted to them. As they neared the temple, Jesus told Chana that she too needed to be careful with what was entrusted to her.

Never had a man spoken to Chana with such compassion.

They didn't go far into the temple. Chana breathed a sigh of relief when Jesus turned to face his followers under Solomon's Porch. He spoke briefly with Simon Peter and two other disciples while everyone else took their seats.

Chana found a spot behind Phyllis and Miriam. She noticed a few other women in the group, most of them older, like herself.

Chana breathed deeply and exhaled slowly. After five or six such breaths, her lightheadedness subsided and her heartbeat returned to normal.

Jesus took a few steps toward the group. "What do you think?" He was saying to them. "A man had two sons."

Chana was thrilled. *He's teaching a parable!* She looked around at the faces in the crowd that were visible to her. None of them seemed to share her excitement. *They've all heard parables before*, she decided. *This is nothing new for them.*

For her, though, it was something close to a lifelong ambition realized. Chana's brother, Othniel, had been a promising rabbinic student in his youth. He excelled at memorizing the Torah and applying its teachings. His interpretive skills were so noteworthy that a local rabbi named Judah deemed Othniel worthy to become his disciple.

As per Jewish custom, Othniel left home to follow Judah in his wanderings. The rabbi taught him Hebrew values and customs. Othniel absorbed every lesson. Judah's interpretations of the law became *his* interpretations. The rabbi's beliefs became *his* beliefs.

When Judah's itinerary brought the rabbi and disciple back to Gennesaret, Othniel would return home to share a meal or an overnight stay with his family. During those visits, he would regale his father with stories of his travels and of Judah's teachings. One of the rabbi's favorite methods of instruction was the parable. Many evenings Chana's father and brother would sit for hours on the roof, trying to unlock the truths hidden in the rabbi's parables.

Chana also would sit for hours—on the exterior staircase, just out of sight—listening to their discussions. Sometimes she marveled at Judah's wisdom. Sometimes she learned something new from her father's and brother's insights. And sometimes she pieced together the meaning of a parable while her father and brother were still wrestling with it.

Chana found she had a certain knack for connecting fictional stories of familiar topics with deeper practical insights. On certain evenings, when she gave her wistfulness a foothold, she wondered what it would be like to sit at a rabbi's feet and listen to his parables in person.

"Here is another parable," Jesus said. "There was a master of the house who planted a vineyard—"

Chana fought back tears of joy.

For a length of time that may have been an hour, or four for all she knew, Chana applied her reasoning skills to parable after parable. She concentrated hard, not just on deciphering the meaning of Jesus's words but on committing each detail to memory. From the great supper to the lost sheep, she didn't want to lose a single image.

The rabbi Judah had died of a fever less than six months after he called Othniel to be his disciple. That put her brother in a terrible limbo. He was not yet trained enough to assume his teacher's position, yet he was too closely aligned with Judah to be called by another rabbi. His dreams of becoming a rabbi died with his teacher.

Years later, Othniel could still recite from memory the words of Judah. Though Chana would never admit it to anyone, she hoped that someday she would be able to do the same with the words of Jesus.

"The kingdom of heaven may be compared to a king who gave a wedding feast for his son—" Jesus said.

Chana drank in his words with a camel's thirst.

Jesus ended his teaching with a brief benediction. The twinge of disappointment Chana felt was quickly replaced by an overwhelming sense of being filled. She told herself that, more than anything in that moment, she needed to be alone. She needed to tame the thoughts that were running wild in her head. She wanted time to absorb every truth she had heard as well as to bask in a joy she had never before experienced. That joy intensified when Phyllis and Miriam turned around. Their eyes were as wide as their smiles.

Miriam squeezed Chana's hands and asked, "What must you be thinking?"

Phyllis reached for her, too, but became distracted by someone or something behind Chana. Chana turned and saw a young woman standing very close to one of the porch columns. The young woman tried to signal the three of them without removing her hands from her cloak. She took a tentative step forward, glanced quickly over her left shoulder and then her right, and retreated back to the pillar.

"What troubles you?" Phyllis called softly to her. She took a few steps toward the young woman. Chana and Miriam followed.

"Forgive me," the young woman said. "I didn't know where else to turn."

"Have you come to be healed from an affliction?" Miriam asked.

The question seemed to confuse the woman. "Healed? No! I would not trouble your teacher in *this* place for such a thing!"

Miriam took a step closer and reached out to the woman, which seemed to unsettle her. The young woman turned her head from side to side, taking in everything in her periphery. Miriam halted her advance.

"I am a servant of Caiaphas," the woman explained. Her voice threatened to buckle under the weight of her words. "I have come with news about your teacher."

"What do you know?" Chana asked.

The woman lowered her voice to a near whisper. "He is in danger. The chief priests and elders are plotting against him. They mean to act soon."

Chana felt a knot tighten in her stomach.

"What do they mean to do?" Miriam asked.

"Caiaphas intends to arrest him and put him on trial. He says your teacher must be made to answer for what he's done."

Phyllis and Chana both turned to Miriam, who nodded and hurried away. The servant seemed slightly unsettled but said nothing.

Miriam weaved through the crowd toward her son-in-law, who was engaged in a heated debate with a group of men. Simon Peter noticed the stricken look on Miriam's face. He turned and tossed a coin in the direction of the men with whom he'd been debating, and hurried after her.

Miriam led him back to where Chana, Phyllis, and the high priest's servant stood. When he saw it was three women who waited for him, he stopped in his tracks.

"What is this news that you bring?" he demanded. He didn't look at the servant. Instead, he focused his gaze on the courtyard beyond Solomon's Porch.

"I have come from the residence of the high priest," the servant explained. "Caiaphas is vexed by your teacher. Even now he is meeting with priests, teachers, and elders to discuss plans to have him arrested and put on trial. This is not the first time they have spoken of such things. Their anger grows. They will not be satisfied until he has been tried by Pilate."

Simon Peter placed his hand over his eyes and rubbed his temples with his thumb and middle finger. He breathed a deep sigh and shook his head. Chana grew uneasy. It was not the reaction of a man who was giving full consideration to the servant's words.

"She has come here at great danger to herself."

Phyllis's helpful reminder did nothing to change the disciple's demeanor. He didn't remove his hand from his eyes.

"The chief priest *and* the Pharisees *and* the Herodians have been searching for a reason to arrest Jesus from the time he first began to teach, years ago." Simon Peter's words were measured and curt. "Their displeasure is nothing new, nor are their threats. But they have found nothing with which they can charge him. Their plots fail, and their wisdom is as foolishness to Jesus. They have not raised an accusation against him that he has not—"

"They desire to arrest him before the Passover celebration ends."

Chana stifled a gasp at the servant's boldness. Her interruption of Simon Peter seemed to catch the disciple off guard.

"Their desires will be their downfall," he replied. "The crowds who welcomed Jesus into the city two days ago—and again today—will not stand idly by if Jesus were taken away, no matter how much he vexes the high priest. *Pilate* would not allow such a thing to happen. *Rome* would not allow such a thing to happen."

He paused for a moment, perhaps expecting another question from the women. None came. He started to walk away, stopped, and turned around. He pulled his cloak open just wide enough to reveal the hilt of his sword. This time, he looked in the women's direction.

"I will tell you one more thing," he said. "I am with him always. I never leave his side. And *I* would not allow such a thing to happen."

The young servant smiled as Simon Peter walked away. "Surely he is a Galilean, for his accent gives him away."

"He is from Bethsaida," Miriam replied.

The servant nodded her head. "My father also was from Bethsaida. He spoke in the same manner."

Phyllis thanked the young woman for risking so much on Jesus's behalf. While they spoke, Chana stepped into the courtyard. Her mind was a whirl of glorious confusion. Questions announced themselves in rapid succession.

What would happen if she followed him as Phyllis and Miriam followed him?

What would Jesus expect from her?

What did she possibly have to give?

Why had his parables impacted her in ways other parables never had?

Why did she feel so offended—and so protective—when she heard that the chief priest was plotting against Jesus?

Why had she been so thrilled when Simon Peter assured them that Jesus would be protected?

Why did she have such concern for someone she had met such a short time earlier?

Though answers did not come quite as quickly, Chana didn't despair. Phyllis had invited her to share the Passover meal at her house, along with other followers of Jesus. Chana felt certain that at least some answers could be found with their help.

Chapter 7

The Meals
Jesus Knew

DIETARY HABITS IN THE 1ST CENTURY AD

In this chapter, we get a glimpse of the dietary habits of people in the first century AD. In first-century China, the diet staples of rice and wheat were supplemented with seafood (shellfish, perch, and bream), game (venison, hare, and turtle) and fowl (chicken, duck, and sparrows' eggs).

The Mayan people of Mesoamerica enjoyed a rich variety of foods. Maize (corn) was the staple of their diet, but they also grew a variety of beans and chilies, as well as sweet potatoes and squash. Their fruits included avocados, watermelon, and papaya. They hunted deer, turkeys, dogs, and wild pigs for meat. They even kept bees for honey.

Their primary morning meal was a porridge made of maize and chilies. During the day, they ate dumplings made of maize dough and filled with meat or vegetables. The dumplings were wrapped with the leaf of a maize plant. Mayan royalty drank chocolate.

The Roman diet was heavily influenced by the eating habits of the Greeks, who believed that wheat bread was the noblest food of all because it was the product of crops grown in a civilized manner by civilized people. Roman soldiers favored wheat bread above all other foods. The bread might be topped with onions, olives, figs, or oil. Such was their mania for wheat bread that they complained bitterly when meat was substituted for it.

This carbohydrate-packed diet caused Roman soldiers to be somewhat heavyset, which was ideal for their purposes. They were expected to stay still and endure when enemies attacked. When mobile, fast-moving troops were required, the Romans recruited them from their barbarian allies.

In contrast to the army, the majority of the Roman population ate very small amounts of wheat. Aside from occasional pork, poultry, fish, and cheese, the average Roman diet was made up almost entirely of vegetables.

Jesus likely ate very well in first-century Israel. The markets of Jerusalem sold everything from fresh vegetables and fruits to fried fish, pickled cucumbers, and freshly grilled meat. More exotic fare could be found at roadside stands, including pickled watermelon rinds and cakes made from chickpeas.

Food also played a key role in first-century Judaism. Significant events in Jewish history were commemorated every year with feasts. Chief among them was Pesach, a sacred celebration that pointed back to the Israelites' deliverance from Egypt when God passed over the Jewish homes, during the killing the Egyptian firstborn on the very first Passover eve.

I n the earliest hours of Passover, the moon found a hiding place behind a bank of clouds and refused to come out. Eli watched it disappear as he stood in line just outside the main gate of the temple.

The orb cast the faintest of glows on the streets of Jerusalem. From Eli's vantage point, a certain trick of the light reminded him of the Sea of Galilee at night. The crowd that spilled out in all directions behind him, gradually receding into the distant darkness, resembled the lake's calm surface. The edges of its boundaries could not be seen, yet there was no mistaking its vastness. As Eli looked out over the mass of humanity, ripples of movement swelled like waves and then disappeared into a noiseless void.

No one spoke a word. Every man who had assembled in the late-night darkness outside the temple stood mute with his Passover sacrifice by his side. The silence of the crowd was disrupted only by the bleating of the lambs.

Eli recalled the first time he waited with his father for the temple gates to be opened—how difficult it had been to stay silent and how his father shook his head every time Eli looked up at him, wordlessly warning his son not to speak. He smiled when he remembered that he had earned the privilege of accompanying his father by beating his brother in a footrace to the city gates when the family's caravan neared Jerusalem.

Eli's reverie was interrupted by the sound of the temple gates being opened. Eli steadied himself as the crowd surged forward in anticipation. Thanks to his early arrival and strategic positioning, he made it through the gate with the first wave of people, just ahead of the bottleneck. Inside the temple courtyard, he did not run. He was no longer that five-year-old boy racing his brother. He strode purposefully across the courtyard to the area where the temple priests would line up in a matter of hours.

Behind him, the courtyard filled with people. When no more could be fit, the temple workers closed the gates. Eli congratulated himself for securing a strategic position for the Passover sacrifice. There were small, but significant, rewards for those who sacrifices were offered first.

The hours between midnight and dawn passed quickly. As the clouds parted to reveal the first rays of morning, a jolt of excitement energized the crowd, and a surge nearly knocked Eli off balance. The temple priests emerged and took their positions, arranging themselves in three human chains. Each chain started at one of the three designated sacrifice areas in the courtyard and stretched all the way to the altar.

Eli admired the skill and efficiency with which they worked—particularly during the Passover sacrifices. Hundreds of thousands of men would pass through the temple courtyards that morning, every one with a lamb for slaughter. The small group of men clad in their priestly attire would make sure that each person returned home having offered an acceptable sacrifice.

The priest at the end of one of the chains stood no more than two shadow lengths away from Eli. When the nearby crowd saw where he had positioned himself, they formed a line facing him. Other sections of the crowd did the same at two other places in the courtyard. The three sacrifice areas were roughly equidistant apart, and the lines that formed at each of them were roughly the same length.

Eli was fourth in his line—a good position, except for the fact that the young man directly in front of him had arrived at the temple *after* Eli. Eli pointed at the lamb of the man in front of him and shook his head. The priest glanced at the animal and then called the first group of about twenty people forward to the sacrifice area.

As the young man in front of Eli approached, the priest kneeled and inspected his lamb. "Where did you purchase your animal?" he asked.

"I bought it from a merchant in the city," the young man replied. "He assured me that it was spotless."

"Why did you trust the word of a merchant when animals from the temple's own flock may be purchased?" the priest asked.

The young man stumbled over his answer.

The priest pointed at his lamb. "This animal has a blemish," he declared. "Leave this place and return when you have an *acceptable* sacrifice."

Eli watched the young man's shoulders slump. He picked up his lamb and walked away, past thousands of pairs of furrowed brows and silently disapproving eyes. Eli positioned himself over his lamb. The priest held a silver cup with a rounded bottom at the ready. With a practiced and steady hand, the priest pulled his knife and drew its blade across the animal's throat. The priest placed the cup under the wound to collect the blood that poured from it. He then moved to the next person in group and repeated the process.

When the cup was filled with each animal's blood, he handed it to the priest behind him, who handed it to the priest behind him. Eventually the cup reached the altar, where the last priest in line poured out its contents.

In the middle of the courtyard, the Levites began to sing the Hallel psalms. Eli picked up his lamb's carcass and hung it from hooks that had been set in the wall for the Passover sacrifice. That the hooks were still available was a testament to Eli's early arrival. The hooks filled quickly, and when they did, people would be forced to hold up one another's sacrifices while the cutting was done. A priest skinned his animal and then opened its abdomen to remove the fatty portions that were required for sacrifice. He placed them in a vessel. Later, a priest would salt the fatty portions before he offered them on the altar.

When his sacrificial duties were done, Eli gathered the animal skin and the meat that remained and placed them in another vessel. As he made his way out of the temple, he noticed that the number of people still waiting in the courtyard to offer sacrifices had dwindled considerably. Soon the gates would be opened again, and the next wave of people would be admitted.

Eli would be long gone by then. He carried the remnants of his sacrifice to the residence of the high priest—the place where he would be partaking of the Passover meal that very evening. Caiaphas himself had extended the invitation.

Caiaphas's servant Malchus answered the door. Eli held out the vessel he was carrying. "Tell your teacher that I have delivered the meat and skin from my sacrifice, to show my appreciation."

"It will be done," the servant replied.

"What will you say to him?" Eli pressed.

"I will tell him that you have delivered the meat and skin from your sacrifice to show your appreciation."

"Who will you say delivered the sacrifice?"

"I will tell him *Eli* delivered the sacrifice," Malchus replied.

Eli stood a little taller at the mention of his name. "See that you do," he said.

Hours later, when he returned to the palatial residence of Caiaphas, Eli's haughtiness had been replaced by giddiness. Few people in Jerusalem—or anywhere, for that matter—could boast of sharing the Passover meal with the high priest of Israel. Malchus answered the door and welcomed him. Another servant washed his feet. When he finished, Malchus led Eli to the formal dining area. A few early arrivals already had gathered. They were mere acquaintances of Eli; none of them possessed any more authority or prestige than he did. He nodded in their direction and then wandered to the opposite side of the room.

The low table in the middle of the dining area was already prepared for the meal. Each place was set with four wine glasses, one plate, and one napkin. On each plate was a small piece of papyrus with a name written on it. Eli was disappointed—and more than a little annoyed—to discover that his place had been set some distance from Caiaphas. He made a mental note of the people who would be seated closer to the high priest.

A bowl of *haroseth*—a sweet sauce made of apples, chopped nuts, red wine, and any number of additional ingredients, depending on the preparer—sat in the middle of the table. Platters of unleavened bread and vegetables flanked the bowl. Next to the bread platter was a bowl of vinegar. Jugs filled with red wine had been placed at the four corners of the table. A dozen or more unlit candles were spaced evenly across the table.

Eli studied the frescoed walls and panels decorated with colored marble. He marveled at the architectural painting positioned perfectly behind the head of the table. Eli intended to have a formal dining room very much like Caiaphas's in his house someday.

The remaining guests were ushered into the room by Caiaphas himself. Everyone washed his hands and took his place at the table. Eli reclined with his left elbow on the pillows that had been set at his place.

Caiaphas looked around at his assembled guests and began. "Blessed are you, O Lord our God, king of the universe, who has created the fruit of the vine—" When the high priest finished the prayer of sanctification, Eli reached for the jug of wine in front of him. He filled his glass and passed the pitcher to his right.

"I am the Lord," Caiaphas recited, "and I will bring you out from under the yoke of the Egyptians."

The guests raised their glasses and drank.

Caiaphas dipped a small stalk of celery into the bowl of vinegar and passed it to his right. He repeated the process until everyone at the table had been served. The chief priest offered a prayer, and everyone at the table partook of the bitter herbs together.

THE WORLD JESUS KNEW

Eli and the other guests poured wine into their second wine glasses. A half dozen servants entered the room and removed the food and drink from the table. The man seated to Caiaphas's left, a minor official in the temple whose name Eli had not bothered to learn, was tasked with asking the ritual questions that preceded the drinking of the second glass of wine.

"Why is this night different from all other nights?" he began.

When his questions were finished, Caiaphas recounted the history of Israel, from the calling of Abraham to their deliverance from slavery in Egypt. With a timing that suggested no small amount of rehearsal, the servants returned just as Caiaphas finished speaking. They placed the food and drink back on the table. They brought with it a large platter of lamb.

Caiaphas pointed to the lamb, the bitter herbs, and the unleavened bread, and he explained the significance of each one. His voice took on a more robust quality as he sang the words, "Praise the Lord. Praise, O servants of the Lord, praise the name of the Lord." He nodded toward his guests, who joined him in song. Together they sang the first half of the Hallel psalms. Their voices echoed in the room after they had finished.

"Blessed are you, O Lord our God, king of the universe, who has created the fruit of the vine," Caiaphas prayed.

Eli and his fellow guests lifted their second wine glasses.

"I will deliver you from their bondage," the high priest recited. The men at the table drank their second glass of wine.

A bowl of water was passed around the table so that the guests could wash their hands, in preparation for the unleavened bread that was about to be broken.

Each man was served a portion of the lamb, a dollop of *haroseth* with vegetables and two wafers of unleavened bread. Caiaphas prayed over the bread and then broke one of the wafers of the priest sitting to his right. Together the two men dipped the broken bread into the *haroseth* and then the vinegar.

The priest then turned to the man on *his* right to repeat the process. After everyone had broken and dipped his bread, the meal began. Eli ate heartily of the portions on his plate. The men ate until only a single wafer of bread remained on their plates. The jugs of wine were passed around again, and the guests filled their third wine glasses.

Caiaphas once again blessed the bread, and the men finished it. Together they recited the post-meal prayer: "The name of the Lord be blessed from now until eternity. Let us bless him of whose gifts we have partaken: Blessed be our God of whose gifts we have partaken, and by whose goodness we exist."

"Blessed are you, O Lord our God, king of the universe, who has created the fruit of the vine."

"I will redeem you with an outstretched arm and with great judgments," Caiaphas recited.

Eli drank his third glass of wine. His fellow guests did the same. They poured the remaining wine in their fourth glasses and together blessed the final glass of wine.

"Then I will take you as my people, and I will be your God; and you shall know that I am the Lord your God, who brought you out from under the burdens of the Egyptians," Caiaphas recited.

The men ended the Passover meal by singing the remainder of the Hallel psalms. Caiaphas allowed the words of the final stanza—"Give thanks to the Lord, for he is good; his love endures forever"—to reach the ceiling.

Chapter 8

The Conflict Jesus Knew

WEAPONRY AND WARFARE IN 1ˢᵀ CENTURY AD

Military might was essential for national survival in the first century AD. Monarchs and rulers who were not prepared to defend every corner of their realm would find themselves vulnerable not only to warlords from within and border-pushing neighbors but also to foreign powers with a taste for empire-building.

In China, rulers of the Han Dynasty enacted strict conscription laws to maintain their military. When a young man reached the age of twenty-three, he was expected to submit to a year of military training. After that, he would serve a year of active duty. When his duty was fulfilled, he remained on semi-active duty. He was allowed to return home but could be called back to training or active service at a moment's notice. Only when he reached the age of fifty-six was he released from his military responsibilities. The only Chinese men who escaped the conscription laws were those whose families could afford to buy exemptions. The primary weapons of the Chinese military were the bow and arrow and the spear and shield. Part of the training process involved regular tests of soldiers' archery skills.

The Mayans of Mesoamerica also featured the bow and arrow in their military campaigns, along with the lance and spear. Other weapons included a war club studded with obsidian edges, a three-pronged claw knife, a flint knife with a broad blade, and an atlatl, which was designed to propel darts and spears at extreme velocities. The Mayans were also infamous for launching hornets' nests into enemy lines. Their defense strategies involved barricades, palisades (high fences made of wooden stakes), and pits with sharp, protruding spikes at the bottom that they dug and hid in strategic places.

The famed Pax Romana, or "Roman Peace," that coincided with the life of Jesus existed only because the Roman army already had demonstrated its military superiority. Roman soldiers carried a short sword (known as a gladius), a javelin (known as a pilum), and a shield. They were trained to march extraordinary distances, abetted by the extensive Roman road system; fight in strategically superior formations; endure extreme conditions; and kill with expert precision. No nation on earth could withstand the might of the Roman legions in the first century AD. Thus, an uneasy peace was established.

The collective military might of Israel in the first century AD was negligible. Centuries of exile and occupation had taken their toll on the ability of the Jewish people to engage their enemies militarily. Some Jewish men served in the Roman military—either voluntarily to gain Roman citizenship or involuntarily because of conscription.

Israelites who did not serve in the military still armed themselves with weapons for many of the same reasons people arm themselves today: to protect themselves, their families, their homes, and their livelihoods. Luke 22:38 makes it clear that two of Jesus's disciples were armed with swords on the night Jesus was arrested. Simon Peter revealed himself to be one of them when he cut off the ear of the high priest's servant in Gethsemane. The Bible offers no clues as to who else was armed that night.

The conversation among Uri's many guests had been continuing, off and on, for two days. Uri had at last revealed to Jared and his brothers that his group, too, was eager to achieve change that would deliver the Jewish people from oppression. After saying this, he had exhorted all three of them to remain cautious and secretive. Failing to do so could cost lives—theirs, or those of their new allies.

The ongoing dialog in Uri's home was sometimes more like a debate, other times an argument. It was trying to determine the best course to take to arrive at the desired change that repeatedly led the group to an impasse.

"Change must begin from *within*," someone insisted, yet again. "Our own priests must return to a single-minded faithfulness to YHWH and overcome any fear—or perhaps it is the *allure*—of Rome."

"Such commitment must begin with the high priest," someone added, emphatically.

Other voices immediately rose in protest. "Those of us who *are* priests are more aware than you of the shortcomings of some of our peers. But attempting to effect change at our level is like trying to stem the flow of the Jordan River as it empties into the Dead Sea. Such an effort must be made much nearer the source, and the source of our problem is the Roman presence in our country. We even know of Pharisees who are willing to do whatever it takes to eliminate this problem—*whatever* it takes. After the Romans are gone, *then* we can effectively deal with corrupt priests."

"I don't know," yet another group member cautioned. "Things could be much worse than they are now. Other than being unable to enforce a death sentence, we have relative freedom to live and worship as we always have. Perhaps it would be better to continue planning, but to postpone conflict of any kind until we see what happens . . . or at least until after the appointment of a new high priest."

Jared was conflicted. On one hand, he was glad to discover that Uri was considering a plan of action. It made good sense to coordinate resources, talents, and effort. On the other, he was frustrated that the assembled group had not agreed to do *something*.

He addressed the group, "Now, while we are all in Jerusalem, is the time to act. If we wait—"

A knock at the door sent Uri's Passover guests scrambling in every direction that offered a makeshift exit from his home. Jared and his brothers crouched near one of the window openings and readied themselves for a quick escape if the situation called for it.

"It is Tirah, a servant of Caiaphas," the voice at the door announced. "I have come with urgent news."

Uri, who stood alone in the middle of the house, signaled for his guests to return to the dining area before he opened the door.

The servant glanced around the interior of the small house before he spoke, as if to confirm the identity of everyone present. "Caiaphas is preparing to arrest Jesus of Nazareth this very night," he announced. "Even now a group is being assembled to find him and make him stand trial."

One of the guests, whose Passover wine had *not* had the alcohol boiled from it, yelled, "What concern is that of ours?"

The room exploded with laughter. Jesus's teachings in the temple had been another topic of conversation around Uri's Passover table.

Uri ignored the laughter. He pointed to Jared and his brothers. "You have been seeking a confrontation since you arrived in Jerusalem," he said. "Tonight you may find one."

The word *confrontation* seemed to catch the attention of the others in the room. The laughter died quickly as the men gathered around Uri.

Jared saw an opportunity. He moved next to Uri and turned to face the group. "The largest fire is lit by a single spark," he proclaimed, "but only if someone fans the flames."

The room went silent. A few of the men glanced at each other in confusion.

"I saw the crowds that greeted this man when he entered Jerusalem," Jared pressed on. "You saw them too. Were there not thousands cheering his arrival? If—*when* –he is arrested, their anger will burn against Rome."

Uri corrected him. "Caiaphas has no need for Rome's help in this matter. He has his own soldiers he can command to do his bidding. The fact that the Nazarene continues to challenge the motives and actions of our own religious leaders is an internal problem—one that the high priest can handle without Roman assistance."

Jared was not convinced. "No. The people on the road-sides were hailing a *king*. Surely Rome will not ignore that kind of talk . . . not for long, at least. They have disposed of rebels for less blatant offenses."

A few men nodded their heads. Jared took that as a sign of progress and continued. "Once this evening has passed, our people's anger will cool. We need to seize this opportunity and fan their anger while it burns; we can spread it throughout Jerusalem."

"The anger of a thousand people is a dangerous weapon," Noam added.

"What would you have us do?" one of the men asked.

"The teacher from Nazareth surrounds himself with disciples," Jared pointed out. "These men never leave his side. Surely they will not stand idly by while he is arrested and taken away."

"It was one of those disciples who came to Caiaphas to arrange for Jesus to be arrested," Tirah the servant interjected.

His interruption sent a ripple of surprise through the room and caused Jared to lose his train of thought. He didn't try to disguise his annoyance.

"Did *all* of Jesus's disciples come to Caiaphas?" Jared asked Tirah through gritted teeth.

"No, just the one," Tirah replied.

"As I was *saying*," Jared continued, "Jesus will be surrounded by followers who will not allow him to be taken without a struggle."

"I have spoken with Simon, one of his disciples who was once very well known to us," Uri said. "He made it clear to me that the others are not warriors. They are fishermen and tradesmen."

Again, murmurs rippled through the crowd. Jared closed his eyes and tried not to react.

"No, they are not warriors," Jared explained slowly. "They may not have the skills, yet surely they will have the desire to protect their teacher. That's why they will need our help. We will do what they *desire* to do but cannot."

"We also have the vision they lack," added Seth. "Perhaps after we rescue the Nazarene teacher, he will see that he can accomplish much more by uniting his thousands of supporters against our common Roman enemy instead of continuing to tell stories and bicker with our religious teachers."

"Caiaphas will surely secure soldiers from Rome before attempting to arrest this teacher," someone interrupted.

"No," Tirah replied. "Caiaphas will handle this internally. He has instructed his servants to recruit a multitude armed with clubs and swords. The arrest party plans to assemble outside of his house."

"A multitude of armed men?" someone muttered. "Against a handful of us?" Angry grumbles followed.

"That is actually good news," Uri said. "First we deal with Caiaphas and his spineless concessions to the empire. Better to face a few temple guards and a crowd of untrained men than Romans who are schooled in fighting techniques and scarred from previous battles. If we start the fight, and continue it, by the time we stand up to Rome, many others should help us finish it. Let us remember that we are not alone. Even now, other groups like ours are forming with similar goals in mind. Perhaps before long we can step out of the shadows and see how many of us there really are!"

Many in the group remained unconvinced.

Uri continued, "And if we die, for what better cause than to declare that YHWH is our king, and not Pilate, or Herod, or Caesar?" Some of the men began to nod slowly.

"We would be remembered for trying to rid our land of tyrants that impose themselves on our lives and worship." Scattered verbal assent could be heard.

"And if we *succeed . . .*" he paused to let that possibility register with the small crowd, ". . . we may even achieve a decisive victory and free the Torah from the defilement of Gentiles."

The buzz of enthusiasm grew louder. Several guests rushed from the house, promising to show up with more weapons—and more supporters. Uri tried to coordinate their movements, instructing the men to arrive from several different directions, so as not to arouse suspicion, and to keep a discreet distance as they followed the arrest party to where Jesus and his disciples were staying.

Tirah returned to the high priest's residence. A short time later, Jared, his brothers, and a few other men quietly followed him. They split into three groups; each took a different route to the house of Caiaphas. Only Uri stayed behind, convinced that his age and slowness of foot would hinder the mission.

Jared found a spot deep in the shadows of a nearby wall and watched as the arresting party assembled. When the number had swelled to several dozen, a man stepped forward to take charge of the group—or at least to try. His words echoed through the porticoes:

"I have brought you here for an important purpose—"

"His disciple and I will approach him first—"

"I will give the signal when you are to—"

Few in the assembled party seemed to pay attention to him. Some nodded absentmindedly while they checked their weapons, torches, and lanterns. Others fidgeted and glanced around, clearly nervous about what they were about to do. Most talked quietly with one another. For the briefest of moments, Jared empathized with their would-be leader.

Eventually he, too, stopped paying attention to the man. His gaze fell on an enormous edifice not an arrow's shot away, and his blood boiled. *The Antonia Fortress.* Ever since he could remember, every time they came to Jerusalem, his father reminded him of how the fortress symbolized the Roman Empire. It towered over the city of Jerusalem the way Rome towered over Israel—always watching, always a threat.

Rome had then become much more than a threat for Jared's family; the omnipresence of the empire was now an all too horrific reality. Jared had not yet turned thirteen when a messenger arrived in Tyre one day with news for their father. His twin brother, their Uncle Caleb, had been killed in Jerusalem.

When their father pressed for details, he discovered that Caleb had come upon two Roman soldiers exercising their right to have a local citizen carry one of their packs for a mile. Uncle Caleb knew the man, and knew that he had great difficulty walking. Caleb tried to volunteer to carry the pack instead, but was told to mind his own business. The Romans either thought the man was being defiant or wanted to teach him a lesson. When Caleb approached again to intervene, one of the soldiers struck him in the head with the hilt of his sword. It was intended as a token show of authority, but the blow was harder than intended. Caleb died the next day.

Jared's father had not been the same since the day he received the news. Week by week he retreated deeper into himself until he became an empty shell of the vigorous man he had been. He made no more trips to Jerusalem for any reason, including Passover. Jared and his brothers had come on their own this year. In the meantime, their local travels had put them in touch with others who were vocal in their opposition to Rome, including the now-disciple Simon. They had found a kindred spirit in Uri, but even he didn't understand their unrestrained rage.

From the time he was old enough to hate, Jared dreamed of launching an assault on the Antonia Fortress and razing it to the ground, destroying it so completely that no two stones would remain stacked on top of one another. If the right leader had approached him on the street at that moment, Jared would follow him—no matter how hopelessly outnumbered they were—into the fortress with his sword in his hand and a battle cry on his lips.

His musings were interrupted as he noticed the arresting party was on the move. In front were the droning leader and another man, whom Jared took to be the traitorous disciple. The rest of the group fell in behind them.

Jared was surprised to see the group exit through the east gate of Jerusalem instead of heading into the city, as he had expected. He stepped from the shadows and waved his arm above his head. Dozens of men emerged from their hiding places. Their ranks had swollen a bit. Good.

They moved cautiously toward the gate, following the lights from the lanterns and torches that proceeded across the Kidron Valley toward the Mount of Olives. Jared and his companions spread out as they trailed the group into the valley. They stayed low to the ground to avoid casting silhouettes in the faint moonlight.

The procession of torches slowed as it reached a small olive grove, known as Gethsemane, at the base of the mountain. The arresting party walked a path that had been cut through the grove. Jared and his group tracked them through the trees on either side of the path.

The arresting party stopped in a small clearing. The torchlights illuminated much of the clearing but did little to penetrate the grove that surrounded them. The disciple, who stood at the front of the group, said something to the leader and then walked a few paces ahead by himself.

Jared positioned himself in a thicket of trees about ten yards away. He raised his hand to a ready position and glanced over his shoulder. In the tree-filtered moonlight, he could make out the shapes of several of his companions, crouched and ready to spring. He hoped the men on the other side of the path were just as prepared.

A man stepped out of the darkness and into the light of the clearing. He did not seem threatened or even surprised at the sudden appearance of the imposing group. Jared couldn't see the man's face clearly but guessed it was Jesus. He was followed by three more men, all of whom shielded their eyes from the light, as if they had just awakened.

"Greetings, teacher!" the traitorous disciple called. He stepped forward and kissed the teacher from Nazareth.

Jesus stared at his disciple for a long moment. The disciple struggled to meet his gaze. "Friend, do what you came to do," Jesus finally said.

Jared could feel his brothers, who were standing closest to him, staring at him through the darkness. He could practically read their thoughts. This was not progressing as they had anticipated.

Four temple guards left their formation and approached Jesus. The bearded, burly disciple who had been standing behind his teacher stepped forward and unsheathed his sword. The suddenness of his movements seemed to catch everyone—including Jared—by surprise. The disciple swung his blade, rather awkwardly, Jared thought, in the direction of the leader.

The intended target managed to fall back far enough to avoid the sword's arc. The man standing next to him, who appeared to be a servant, was not so lucky. He spun away from the blow so fast that he nearly lost his balance, then raised both hands to the left side of his head. No one else in the group moved. They all stared at something on the ground in front of them.

The first blow has been struck! Jared realized.

He turned to give the signal to his companions, but his brother Noam grabbed his arm before he could. Noam pointed to the clearing, where Jesus was bent over, picking up something from the ground.

A tree branch obstructed Jared's view, but it appeared that Jesus placed his hand near the injured man's wound. Someone in the arresting party gasped. Several of them took a few steps backward, away from Jesus. The injured man rubbed his left ear, as though he'd never felt it before.

Jesus pointed to his armed disciple. "Put your sword back into its place," he commanded. "For all who take the sword will perish by the sword. Do you think that I cannot appeal to my Father, and he will at once send me more than twelve legions of angels? But how then should the Scriptures be fulfilled, that it must be so?"

From the cover of the olive grove, Jared stared in confusion and disbelief.

Jesus turned and pointed to the weapons being wielded by those who had come to arrest him. "Have you come out as against a robber, with swords and clubs to capture me? Day after day I sat in the temple teaching, and you did not seize me. But all this has taken place that the Scriptures of the prophets might be fulfilled."

The leader regained his composure after his near decapitation. He said something Jared couldn't hear to the guards, who stepped forward and grabbed Jesus by the arms and shoulders. He offered no resistance.

The three disciples who accompanied Jesus did not wait around to see what happened next. Two of them bolted in the direction from which they had come. The other—the sword wielder—made for the trees on the opposite side of the clearing from Jared and his men. The leader of the arrest party shook his head as he watched the disciples disappear into the darkness.

"You did not choose your disciples for their courage, did you?" one of the priests in the crowd asked Jesus. The teacher from Nazareth said nothing as he was led out of Gethsemane and back to Jerusalem.

After the arrest party had departed the olive grove, Jared and his companions emerged from the trees.

"Cowards are not deserving of our help," someone muttered.

"All is not yet lost," Jared replied. "Once the shock of their teacher's arrest has passed, these disciples may yet prove to be courageous."

Chapter 9

The Law Jesus Knew

LEGAL SYSTEMS
IN 1ˢᵀ CENTURY AD

Laws and judicial systems in our modern world may differ when it comes to procedures, nuances, and emphases, but basic commonalities can be found in the twenty-first-century law books of North America, Europe, and Asia. Such was not the case in the world Jesus knew.

Chinese law during the Han Dynasty of the first century AD was based on the belief that all parts of the universe— humans, nature, everything—are interdependent. The Chinese believed that the actions of humankind directly affected the physical world. They believed natural phenomena such as floods and drought were caused by imbalances in the human-nature relationship. It was essential, then, that human laws took into account the interdependence of the universe. Crimes had to be counterbalanced by punishment, lest the balance of the universe be affected. Death sentences had to be carried out in autumn and winter, the seasons of death and decay in nature.

The batab, or local village chieftain, was central to the legal system of the Mayans in Mesoamerica. He settled judicial disputes among the people in his village. His wisdom and judgment were unassailable. His rulings were the law among his people. The batab also carried out the oracles of the priests—especially as they related to sowing, reaping, and celebrating as a village.

Roman law separated itself from all others by virtue of the Twelve Tables. Whereas other nations were governed by the whims and arbitrary judgments of kings, priests, and chieftains, Rome had a ten-man commission that codified rules—supposedly for everyone, though the wealthy and privileged usually found ways around them. By putting laws into books, Roman legal authorities created a system that was accessible and discoverable to all citizens.

The Sanhedrin was the supreme religious and civil ruling body in Israel. Jewish law consisted first of the written Torah, the first five books of the Old Testament, which contain legal rules as well as stories from which additional rules can be drawn. The second part of Jewish law was the oral Torah, the legal traditions of the Jewish people. Because they were oral, as opposed to written, these legal traditions were open to various interpretations. The responsibility for determining the correct interpretation in a given situation fell to the Sanhedrin.

Established in 191 BC, the Sanhedrin served as the Jewish high court and legislature. The body consisted of a president (nasi), vice-president (av bet din), and sixty-nine members, who sat in a semicircle facing the leaders. In legal matters, the group questioned the accused, the accusers, and witnesses before rendering their decisions. In matters of religious law, the group resolved disagreements by majority vote.

Around AD 28, the Sanhedrin was stripped of its right to try capital offenses. That complicated matters when Jesus of Nazareth was brought before them after his arrest. The Jewish authorities required six different trials—three with the Jewish courts and three with Roman authorities in order to convict and sentence him to death.

"A prophet who seeks the company of women, Samaritans, and tax collectors is no potential messiah! He should be *arrested*!"

The voice of Chana's brother chased her from his home. She struggled to carry a large bag made of goatskin to the front door. Her bag, which contained all of her earthly possessions, meager as they were, grew larger and heavier with every step. She tried to say goodbye to her sister-in-law and nephew, but they could neither see nor hear her, even though she was right in front of them. She managed to pull her bag through the doorframe just before the door slammed behind her. The word *arrested* echoed as she walked away.

Chana sat up in bed. The details of her nightmare drifted away like tendrils of smoke from an extinguished candle. What remained was the realization that never again would she be welcome in her brother's house. The faint moonlight illuminated a narrow strip from the window to the doorway of Phyllis' guestroom. Beyond the doorway, Chana could see shadows cast by the glow of a lantern and could hear muffled voices carrying on an urgent conversation.

"—arrested."

"Arrested?"

Chana moved quietly to the doorway and peered out. Near the front door of the house, Phyllis was standing with her back to Chana, facing Abigail, the young servant of Caiaphas whom Chana had met earlier in the temple. Phyllis had her hands on Abigail's shoulders, as though she were trying to calm the young servant. A flickering lantern hung nearby on the wall.

Abigail spotted Chana standing in the doorway. "Jesus has been arrested—just as I warned you he would be!" she cried. The words poured from her so quickly that Chana struggled to make sense of them. "He has been taken to Annas to stand trial. After that, he will be taken to Caiaphas."

Chana's knees buckled. She grabbed the doorframe for support.

Phyllis turned to Chana. "You will return with Abigail to the high priest's residence. Abigail says you may warm yourself beside a fire in the courtyard. I will gather the others and then join you. If we hurry, we may yet see the teacher tonight."

As promised, a bonfire burned in the center of the upper courtyard of Caiaphas's residence. A long vestibule led from the courtyard to the front door. The vestibule was bordered on one side by the dining room, with its frescoed walls, and on the other side by the reception hall, where Jesus stood trial. The sleeping quarters on the second floor of the residence were apparently vacant tonight.

Outside, a stone staircase at the southwest corner of the courtyard led to a lower courtyard. This small open area was bordered by a *mikvah,* a bathing area where priests ritually cleansed themselves, and a vaulted storeroom.

In the upper courtyard, several people were gathered around the fire, trying to stave off the evening chill. Abigail hurried into the house to see if anyone had noted her absence. It seemed no one had. She returned to the fire and stood next to Chana.

"Jesus is already here," she whispered. "The trial has begun."

Chana said nothing. For a long time, she simply stared into the fire.

The sound of footsteps approaching from the vestibule roused her from her thoughts. A well-dressed man, illuminated by torches that stood on either side of the entrance to the vestibule, stopped at the courtyard's edge and peered out at the gathering near the fire.

The smile on his lips gave Chana a moment of hope—but she shuddered when she got a closer look. She had seen such smiles on boys when she was a young girl—boys who were always up to no good. It was especially disturbing to see the same expression on a full-grown man.

An older man, also dressed in fine clothes, approached the smiling younger man. His expressionless face made it clear that he was no more fooled by the smile than was Chana. She was just able to hear their conversation.

"If justice cannot be found among those to whom it has been entrusted, then where can justice be found?" the older man began.

"Who am I to answer the questions of the learned, Joseph?" The smile did not leave the young man's lips.

"Are you not a priest? Joseph asked. "Are you not Eli, the one who led the arrest party?"

"I carried out the orders of the high priest."

"You violated Jewish law."

The smile vanished from Eli's lips.

"Were you not taught that the law prohibits authorities from arresting or trying criminals at night?" Joseph asked. "Have the morning sacrifices been offered?"

Eli looked away.

"Have the morning sacrifices been offered?" Joseph pressed.

"No."

"Were you not taught that the Sanhedrin is not to assemble until the hour after the morning sacrifice?" The old man did not raise his voice, but his tone grew more intense. The people sitting near the fire turned to face the two men, whose every word they could hear.

"How many other laws have been violated this night—this *Passover* night, when no judgment is to be issued?" Joseph continued.

"He was judged guilty by every member of the Sanhedrin," Eli countered.

Chana gasped. *Judged guilty.* The trial was over.

"Did the accused call witnesses on his own behalf?" Joseph asked. He seemed especially troubled by this news.

Eli could not resist rubbing salt in the wound. "Not one."

"Then he cannot be found guilty," the old man pointed out. "An accused man may have at least two witnesses at his trial."

Chana glanced around at the faces illuminated by the bonfire to see how the other spectators reacted to the men's exchange. Few betrayed any rooting interest.

"You probably know little of the high priest's hatred for Jesus of Nazareth," Joseph said to Eli.

"I know more of his hatred than *you* do," Eli snapped. "For years the man has kindled Caiaphas's anger. And in that time Caiaphas has wisely determined that, should he be convicted, it is ultimately for the good of the people."

Joseph nodded and said, "Tell me, then, what kind of legitimate court allows a judge to be an enemy of the one who is accused?"

Someone in the courtyard—someone beyond the glow of the fire—chuckled. Eli heard it and took a step in that direction. He looked out into the darkness and realized he should have known better than to publicly debate the reputable Joseph of Arimathea. He would take another tactic. His eerie smile returned.

"You are a learned man, Joseph," Eli said, "certainly more learned than I." He didn't turn back to the old man. Instead, he directed his words to the people in the courtyard, as a Roman politician would do. "So perhaps you can tell me this: Where will a man of your integrity and righteous character take his objections? Where will he lodge his complaints?"

Chana waited eagerly for the old man's reply, but none came.

Eli turned, whispered something in Joseph's ear, and then walked back through the vestibule to the reception room. Joseph stood in place, his head bowed slightly. After a moment, he looked up and saw his fellow guests in the courtyard staring at him. He shook his head, walked slowly through the vestibule, and left the building.

Chana wiped the tears from her eyes. Abigail placed her hand on Chana's shoulder and leaned close to whisper in her ear. "Caiaphas does not have the power to condemn a prisoner to death. Only Pilate can do that. There is still hope that—"

Chana turned and saw Abigail staring open-mouthed at someone across the bonfire. Chana couldn't see the man clearly from where she sat due to the flames and the fact that he was sitting behind a group of people.

"Who—"

Abigail stood and brushed past her before she could finish her question. "You were with Jesus the Galilean!" the servant girl cried as she approached the man. As the crowd turned, the light from the bonfire briefly illuminated his face before he covered his face with his hand. In that brief moment, in the semidarkness of the courtyard, Chana recognized Simon Peter.

She jumped to her feet and followed Abigail.

The burly disciple reacted like a thief who had been caught stealing. His eyes went wide, and he looked around quickly to see if anyone else was approaching. He slowly backed away from the women, without giving any indication that he recognized them.

"I saw you when you spoke to Caiaphas's servant. You said you would stay with him to the end." Chana spoke so quietly that no one else but Abigail and Simon Peter could hear her. "You said you would never leave his side. You said you would never allow him to be arrested."

Her words seemed to trigger something in Simon Peter's memory. The sadness that clouded his eyes was too much for Chana to bear. She had to look away. A few other people around the bonfire stood up and approached the disciple. The movement seemed to rattle him.

"I do not know what you are talking about," he told the women.

Chana stared at him, silently pleading for him to do something—anything—to save Jesus. He would not meet her gaze. He kept his eyes focused on the vestibule.

Crouched on the stairway at the southwest corner of the courtyard, Jared muttered a curse when the servant girl recognized Simon Peter. He wanted to see what the disciple would do with the element of surprise on his side.

Jared had spotted Simon Peter walking alone after the standoff at Gethsemane. Jared still hoped that Jesus's followers were ripe for insurrection, despite their cowardice in the olive grove. Only Simon Peter had demonstrated a willingness to fight. If his teacher had not stopped him, he might have incited a riot—one that Jared and his companions would have joined.

From such riots, rebellions are born, Jared reminded himself.

The disciple still carried his sword—and Jared still saw potential in him, even if the rest of Uri's associates did not. Jared had followed the disciple back to Jerusalem, where he made his way to the high priest's residence.

For just a moment, Jared wondered if the disciples had a plan to free Jesus. Given their actions in Gethsemane, the likelihood seemed remote. A quick surveillance of the courtyard made it seem even more unlikely. There was no sign of any disciple, aside from Simon Peter, outside the high priest's residence. If he planned to act, he was going to do it alone— and that would be of no use to Jared. He had gotten a glimpse of the disciple's sword skills in the olive grove. The man would almost certainly be captured or killed before he could inflict much injury to the people who had arrested his teacher.

As far as Jared was concerned, Simon Peter's value lay in his leadership potential—people seemed to follow him. That was the message he intended to convey to the disciple when he saw that he was still loyal to his teacher. Unfortunately, the servant girl's outburst had made Jared's task much more difficult. She had drawn attention to Simon Peter, which was the last thing the disciple wanted in this setting.

Even from across the courtyard, Jared could see Simon Peter was rattled. He needed to be reminded of who he was. Jared stepped out of the shadows and slowly approached the disciple. He didn't want to scare him or make him think someone was coming for him.

As he got closer, Jared could hear the woman who was with the servant girl speaking quietly to Simon Peter, reminding him of his responsibilities as a follower of Jesus. Her strategy seemed sound.

"You are one of them too!" Jared called out.

Simon Peter turned in his direction. He scanned the darkness behind Jared as though he expected others—perhaps the high priest's armed guards—to emerge from it.

Jared took a few more cautious steps. He pointed to the servant girl, the woman next to her, and others in the courtyard to try to convince the disciple that he was among allies. He tapped his own sword and then nodded toward Simon Peter's to drive home his point.

After a moment's confusion, the disciple seemed to piece together Jared's meaning. He glanced down at his sword and then shook his head at Jared.

"Man, I am not!" he said. The truth had become clear to Peter in that smoky courtyard. He had indeed been ready to defend his teacher to the death, but it wasn't an armed mob that stopped him. It was Jesus himself. He had misunderstood and let Jesus down . . . and it wasn't the first time. The realization was almost more than he could bear. The emphasis of his second denial caused the older woman to start weeping.

Eli's mentor taught him always to pause just outside the doorway when he left a room so that he could hear what was being spoken about him. That instinct served him well in the courtyard of the high priest. After his confrontation with Joseph of Arimathea, Eli sneaked back to the vestibule and hid behind a column.

None of the conversations he overheard concerned *him*, much to his disappointment. However, one exchange did confirm a suspicion he held. The servant girl, in her ignorance and carelessness, had revealed the presence of one of Jesus's disciples. Eli couldn't see the man from his hiding place, but he kept watching.

The man who had then approached the unidentified disciple in the courtyard caught Eli off guard. Eli had encountered more than his share of dissidents during his time with Jesus, and this was undoubtedly one of them. The Nazarene spoke consistently of peace, yet some of those who followed him sniffed around like dogs, looking for something to fight over. When they found nothing, they moved on. Always plotting rebellion and trying to recruit others, they never seemed to *accomplish* anything, as far as Eli could tell. They could usually be found skulking in the shadows and brandishing their weapons.

Perhaps the disciple he couldn't see was Simon, the only one of the Nazarene's followers (that he knew of) with past ties to those critical of Rome. For nearly an hour, the aggressive stranger appeared to be trying to convince the disciple of something, but to no avail. Then, for just a moment, the crackling of the fires and the sound of the wind silenced enough for him to hear a phrase or two of the conversation.

He still couldn't see the disciple, but he knew that voice! He had last heard it when the disciple had humiliated him on the road from Bethany to Jerusalem, commanding him to empty his coin pouch. Two days ago it had been an arrogant, demanding voice. Judging by the panic in that voice now, however, Simon Peter was a man ripe for torment. Clearly, all of the fight had left him back in the olive grove.

Eli stepped out of the shadows and approached the cowering disciple. The unidentified dissident saw him coming and retreated to the back staircase. Others, who had surrounded the disciple, backed off a bit, but they did not turn away. Simon Peter immediately recognized Eli, but didn't move. He watched helplessly as the smirking priest approached, clearly savoring the moment.

"Certainly this man also was with him," Eli announced in a loud voice, "for he is a Galilean too."

"Man, I do not know what you are talking about," Peter cried. He unleashed a torrent of curses, swearing that he did not know Jesus.

Eli was planning to make the most of this opportunity, but it was over all too soon. In his peripheral vision, he caught sight of four figures surrounding a fifth, all making their way down a flight of stairs that led from the reception hall to the small storage rooms that doubled as temporary jail cells.

In the distance, a rooster crowed.

Eli watched as Simon Peter and Jesus locked eyes for the briefest moment before the Nazarene and his temple guards disappeared from view. But that was long enough. The timing was perfect, better than any retaliation Eli could ever have exacted.

The color drained from Simon Peter's face. He doubled over as though someone had struck him in the stomach. Tears swelled in his eyes as a low, guttural moan seemed to come from deep within him. He rose quickly, stumbled to the staircase, and started down. The receding sounds of his anguished cries marked his descent.

As dawn broke over the residence of Caiaphas, the high priest, a small group of people near a bonfire in the courtyard stared at one another in confusion and surprise. A servant girl and an older woman clung to one another, both of them weeping. And a well-dressed temple worker stood with his hands on his hips, staring in the direction of the back staircase. The satisfied smile on his face suggested that he had just won an important victory.

Chapter 10

The Currency
Jesus Knew

CURRENCY AND COINS IN 1ST CENTURY AD

The proliferation of foreign trade in the first century AD created an urgent need for coins and currency—items of specific value that could be exchanged for goods and services. In China, efforts to establish a stable currency system were undermined by the production of a succession of coins of differing values, many of which were pulled from circulation or replaced just a year or two after they were introduced. Discrepancies between the face value of coins and their actual weight added to the confusion.

Chinese coins typically were made of bronze; they were round, with a square hole in the middle of the coin. In addition to coins, the Chinese used gold, silver, tortoise shells, knives, hemp, silk, and grain as currency.

The Egyptians of the first century AD—who, like the people of Israel, were under Roman rule—maintained a closed currency system. Their coins rarely circulated outside of Egypt's borders. Likewise, foreign coins rarely found their way into the country's currency. One exception was the silver tetradrachma, an ancient Greek currency that was the primary coin of Roman-controlled Egypt during the time of Jesus.

The silver denarius held that distinction in Rome. The denarius was the equivalent of a day's wage for a laborer or soldier. Julius Caesar, the first Roman emperor, recognized the power that lay in the minting of coins. He broke with tradition by issuing coins with his own image on them. His successors followed suit.

The people of Israel dealt with a variety of coins in their daily commerce. Jerusalem was a popular tourist destination and a common stop for caravans and various trade routes, so the city was flooded with foreign currency. This proved problematic when it came to monetary matters concerning the temple. Coins that depicted an earthly ruler were considered idolatrous and could not be used to pay the required temple tax. Therefore, Roman and other foreign coins had to be exchanged for Tyrian coins, which depicted no earthly ruler. The Jewish temple was filled with moneychangers who charged for their services—much to Jesus's displeasure.

Coins figure prominently in the Bible's account of Jesus's ministry. In Luke 15, Jesus teaches a parable of a lost coin that is found to illustrate the joy of redemption. In Mark 12, he notices rich people placing large sums of money in the temple treasury, followed by a poor widow who offers only two small copper coins, worth practically nothing by comparison. Jesus praised the woman's sacrifice over those of the rich people because she gave everything she had.

Perhaps the most notorious link between Jesus and the currency of his day comes courtesy of the apostle Judas Iscariot, who was paid thirty pieces of silver for betraying Jesus into the hands of his enemies.

Eli did not relish the role of messenger. He believed the job was beneath him, a waste of his talents, a task better suited for servants. He did relish his standing with Caiaphas, who believed that some messages were too important to be left to servants. Eli enjoyed his prominence among the religious elite of Jerusalem. So if maintaining that standing and prominence meant occasionally delivering a message to the priests of the temple that Jesus would be taken to Pilate, the Roman governor, to stand trial, Eli was only too willing to comply.

He found the chief priests in the outer courtyard, standing with a group of elders near a moneychanger's table. He greeted the men and then filled them in on the previous night's proceedings, placing particular emphasis on his encounter with Joseph of Arimathea. His message regarding Jesus's trial before Pilate was interrupted by a bedraggled man who seemed to search the courtyard before he caught sight of Eli and the priests and elders.

The man walked straight toward them, without a glance to his left or right. Several other temple visitors had to step quickly to get out of his way. He stopped some distance from Eli and his companions and held up two small bags. His arms strained to keep them aloft.

Eli recognized the bags and then the man. "Judas Iscariot," he said quietly to his companions.

"Who is he?" one of them whispered.

"The disciple who betrayed the Galilean."

"I have sinned by betraying innocent blood!" Judas cried.

The laughter came fast and cruel. "What is that to us?" one of the elders replied. "See to it yourself!"

The guilt-stricken disciple heaved the two bags in the men's direction, and the laughter stopped. Both bags burst open. Silver coins—thirty of them in all—spilled on the floor at the men's feet. Judas left as quickly and as purposefully as he had arrived. No one tried to stop him. No one tried to follow him.

Two of the priests sent for their servants, who hurried to the scene and began picking up the coins and putting them back in the bags. Eli picked up one of the coins himself and turned it over and over in his hand.

"It is not lawful to put these into the treasury," one of the priests warned. "It is blood money."

Someone else suggested using the coins to buy the potter's field in the city so that it could be used as a burial place for strangers and visitors. Eli glanced at the coin in his hand. A profile image of Caesar Augustus stared back at him. He tossed the coin into one of the bags. The discussion regarding what to do with the money grew heated, so Eli took his leave.

He arrived back at the high priest's residence just as the prisoner was being led away. The priests led the procession. They were followed by Jesus, whose hands were bound, surrounded by four temple guards. Bringing up the rear was an assortment of elders, teachers of the law, and temple workers.

An early morning chill hung over the city as the group made the short walk north to the western edge of the city. Pilate, the Roman governor, insisted on staying at Herod's opulent palace when he visited Jerusalem. The enormous structure stood adjacent to the towers of Phasael, Hippicus, and Mariamne, just south of the Gennath Gate.

The streets already were starting to fill. Several passersby stopped to stare as the Jewish religious leaders paraded their prisoner to Pilate.

"Jesus of Nazareth!" someone called from a nearby roof.

"Days ago, this man was greeted as a king when he rode into the city," another man remarked to no one in particular.

Eli noticed a few people scurry away, undoubtedly to tell their friends—or perhaps even the Galilean's disciples—what they had seen.

Palace officials greeted the delegation at the entrance to the complex and invited the men inside.

"Tell the governor that our law forbids us from entering this dwelling," one of the priests told them. "Therefore, we request his presence outside to settle an urgent matter of law."

The request was not unusual. Pilate had accommodated Jewish law in similar situations in the past. Yet the palace officials seemed reluctant to take the message to the governor. Eli wondered if it was because they were new to their positions, or because they knew Pilate was in no mood to deal with such matters.

"If we enter the home of a Gentile, we will be made ceremonially unclean," an elder explained. "We will be unable to partake of our remaining Passover meals."

The officials agreed to deliver the message to the governor. A short time later, Pilate emerged from the palace. His wife and a few Roman officials were with him. Pilate regarded the Jewish delegation as an exasperated parent might regard his misbehaving children. He shook his head and rubbed his hand over his face.

"What accusation do you bring against this man?" he asked.

Eli could sense his irritation, as could the priest who answered him. "If this man were not doing evil, we would not have delivered him over to you," he assured Pilate.

"Take him yourselves and judge him by your own law," Pilate insisted.

"It is not lawful for us to put anyone to death," the priest reminded him.

The Roman governor studied the prisoner for a moment and then looked back at the man's accusers. His confusion was apparent.

Behind the delegation of priests, teachers, and elders, a small crowd began to form. The presence of these newcomers seemed to transform Pilate's demeanor. He stood more erect. His face took on a less irritated and more thoughtful expression. He projected a more gubernatorial manner.

"We found this man misleading our nation, disturbing our religious practices, and challenging our authority," a teacher of the law called to Pilate, prompting whispers from the crowd. He added, "He also causes trouble in the temple and claims to be a king and suggests his kingdom is greater than Rome's," which resulted in a considerably louder response.

Pilate signaled for the soldiers to escort Jesus into the palace. He and his entourage followed them. Eli and the rest of Jesus's accusers waited outside the palace with the ever-growing crowd.

One of the elders in the group called the rest of the men to himself. He spoke in a low voice so that his words would not be overheard. "Pilate will soon honor the Passover tradition of releasing one of our prisoners to us." He pointed to the growing mob. "How many of these people will be sympathetic to the Galilean and demand his release?"

Eli silently chastised himself for not anticipating that situation. If Jesus were released at the behest of the crowd, all of Eli's efforts—all his clandestine work among the Galileans—would have been for naught.

"They must be persuaded otherwise," one of the priests urged. He turned to the crowd and pointed to the palace entrance where Jesus was taken. "This Galilean has profaned the Passover with his blasphemy," he shouted. "He claims to be David's king, the one to lead the nation into restoration."

The crowd stirred a little but otherwise did not react to his words.

Eli chose a more direct strategy. He approached a man in the crowd, looked him in the eye, and said, "Pilate will soon ask which Jewish prisoner he should release in honor of the Passover season." He intensified his stare. "He must *not* release the Galilean, Jesus of Nazareth."

The man nodded, clearly rattled by Eli's words.

Others in Eli's group followed his example, pulling aside individuals to offer veiled warnings. They were interrupted by the reappearance of Pilate, Jesus, and the soldiers.

"I find no guilt in this man," Pilate declared.

The priests, elders, and teachers of the law erupted, launching a cacophony of charges and accusations against Jesus. No single voice could be heard above the din. The vehemence of the reaction seemed to startle the Roman governor.

"Have you no answer to make?" he asked Jesus. "See how many charges they bring against you." The Galilean stared at his accusers but offered no reply, no defense, and no explanation. Pilate shook his head in disbelief.

Eli rushed back to the crowd and pointed at Jesus. "His silent tongue is proof of his guilt!" he cried.

One of the priests held up his hands to calm his companions. He stepped forward and said, "He stirs up the people, teaching throughout Galilee even to this place."

Pilate stopped him before he could say more. "Is this man a Galilean?" he asked. Eli and his companions nodded.

Pilate threw up his hands. "His crimes fall under the jurisdiction of Herod. But do not be discouraged. Fortune has smiled upon you today because Herod is in residence as we speak." He pointed to the palace of Herod Antipas, which stood just a short distance away. The ruler of Galilee had traveled to Jerusalem for Passover from his primary palace in Tiberias, the capital city he built for himself on the western shore of the Sea of Galilee.

The Jewish religious leaders marched Jesus to Herod's opulent residence. Palace officials led the group to Herod's royal chamber. Unlike Pilate, the Jewish king seemed glad to see Jesus. Eli's heart sank.

"I have heard much about you," Herod told Jesus. "I am told that you perform signs and wonders."

"He performs the work of demons," one of the elders muttered loud enough for everyone to hear.

Herod ignored the interruption. "Show me a sign now," he instructed. "I have heard the people say you can multiply food or, even better, turn water into wine. Do something to make me believe, and I will set you free."

His offer prompted another outburst from Eli's companions. They lobbed accusations concerning Jesus's blasphemy, his penchant for stirring up unrest among his followers, and the peoples' recent acknowledgement of him as David's king. Eli kept his eyes on Jesus while they shouted their charges. He stared at each man who spoke but said nothing himself.

Herod grew angry at Jesus's refusal to obey his instructions or answer his questions. He began to taunt the prisoner, asking him why the king of the Jews dressed like an ordinary villager.

Herod's soldiers soon joined in the taunting. One of them held up a scarlet robe. "A garment fit for a king!" he exclaimed. He placed the robe over Jesus's shoulders while his fellow soldiers roared with laughter.

Herod seemed to tire quickly of the merriment. "Remove him from my sight," he commanded.

Eli and his companions looked at one another, uncertain of what to do next. The tone of the king's command did not invite questions or objections. They trudged back to see Pilate with their silent prisoner in tow.

The crowd outside had doubled in size in just the short time Eli and his companions had stood before Herod. Eli felt a swell of pride when several of the elders, teachers of the law, and temple workers approached the crowd, just as he had done, to turn people against the Galilean.

One of the elders approached three young men—probably brothers, based on their resemblance to one another—who seemed to be taking an unusually strong interest in Jesus's predicament.

"Have you considered how his followers might react to his death?" one of them asked.

The elder confessed that he hadn't considered such a thing.

Neither the elders nor the teachers of the law nor the temple workers bothered to approach a group of older women who had gathered directly behind Jesus. Some of the women were crying; others were waving their hands as though they were trying to get Jesus's attention.

The crowd quieted when Pilate emerged from his palace. He looked at Jesus and shook his head.

"You brought me this man as one who was misleading the people," he said to the religious leaders. "And after examining him before you, behold, I did not find this man guilty of any of your charges against him. Neither did Herod, for he sent him back to us. Look, nothing deserving death has been done by him. I will therefore punish and release him."

Eli and his companions, along with many in the crowd, roared their disapproval.

Pilate continued, and the roar ceased. "I find no guilt in him," he repeated. "But you have a custom that I should release one man for you at the Passover. So do you want me to release to you the King of the Jews?"

Eli glanced at his companions, who scowled at the governor's choice of titles. The crowd reaction was swift and decisive. "Not this man, but Barabbas!" several shouted in unison. Others simply chanted the name, "Barabbas!"

Barabbas was a notorious insurrectionist who been arrested for committing murder. Having him released from prison undoubtedly would seem like a victory to his fellow rebels. Eli looked at Jesus and wondered how one man could unite the religious elite of Jerusalem and the basest criminals in Israel in a common pursuit.

A small chorus of voices rose in counterpoint to the majority. Eli allowed himself to relax when he heard it. The voices were female. The only vocal supporters Jesus had left were women.

Pilate brushed past Eli as he made his way to the Stone Pavement (or Judgment Seat), an elevated stone platform from which he issued his rulings. As soon as he sat down, a royal official approached him. "I have a message from your wife," he said. Though he put his face close to Pilate's ear, he had to speak loudly to be heard over the crowd noise. Eli stood close enough to hear the official's every word, though he pretended not to hear a thing.

"What is the message?" Pilate asked.

"Have nothing to do with that righteous man, for I have suffered much because of him today in a dream."

Pilate stared at the official for a moment, as though he expected more. The man offered only a slight bow before he backed away. Pilate closed his eyes and pinched the bridge of his nose.

"What shall I do with Jesus?" he asked the crowd.

"Let him be crucified!" came the reply. The cries for execution mingled with the muffled sounds of women—and a few men—weeping.

"Why? What evil has he done?" the governor pressed.

"Let him be crucified!" the crowd repeated.

"Take him yourselves and crucify him, for I find no guilt in him." Pilate's tone suggested that his patience was being tested.

One of the teachers answered him. "We have a law, and according to that law he ought to die because he has made himself the Son of God."

His words seemed to rattle Pilate, who shifted in his seat. He ordered a royal official to bring him a bowl of water. He stood, dipped his hands into the water, and began to wash them.

"I am innocent of this man's blood," he told the crowd. "See to it yourselves."

The crowd cheered, but Eli did not join their celebration. His concentration was fixed on the prisoner who was being led back into Pilate's palace by a squadron of Roman soldiers eager to spill his blood. The sentenced man should have been pleading for mercy, or distraught, or hopeless.

Yet the Galilean showed no trace of anger, fear, or panic as the door closed behind him. Instead, he seemed almost at peace with his fate. Eli shut his eyes tightly, but the image would not leave him.

Chapter 11

The Justice System
Jesus Knew

CRIME AND PUNISHMENT
IN 1ST CENTURY AD

Capital punishment was deeply entrenched in the legal system of virtually every nation on earth in the first century AD. The Ancient Laws of China, the earliest recorded legal documents in Chinese history, identified specific capital crimes. The Code of Hammurabi, the ancient Babylonian king, had been around since about 1750 BC and prescribed the death penalty for twenty-five different offenses—none of which, curiously enough, included murder.

The first historically recorded death sentence comes from Egypt in the sixteenth century BC. A nobleman accused of practicing magic was ordered to commit suicide. Two centuries later, the Code of the Hittites included provisions for the death penalty. The Draconian Code of Athens in the seventh century BC took capital punishment to its extreme by requiring the death penalty for every crime.

In Rome, from the fifth century BC onward, the Law of the Twelve Tablets prescribed the death penalty for several different offenses, including adultery, counterfeiting, and giving false witness. Enforcement of the Roman death penalty was reserved almost exclusively for criminals of a lower class, including slaves and non-citizens of Rome. Citizens in the upper classes of Roman society who were convicted of capital crimes were exiled or had their property seized. If the

crime were serious enough, the person was given the oppor-
tunity to commit suicide.

Capital punishment had been part of Jewish law from the
earliest days of Israel. The Old Testament identifies three dif-
ferent methods for putting wrongdoers to death: stoning (the
most common method), burning, and hanging. In the early
first century, it was left to the Sanhedrin (see introduction
to chapter 9) to determine which offenses were punishable by
death. Sometime before Jesus was put on trial, however, the
Roman government revoked the Sanhedrin's authority to try
capital cases. In order to put Jesus to death, Jewish religious
leaders required the cooperation of Pilate, the Roman governor.

The Romans were particularly cruel in their execution
methods. In addition to burying people alive or throwing
them from cliffs, they devised the poena cullei ("the penalty of
the sack"), in which a prisoner was bound and placed in a
sack made of ox skin, along with a rooster, a dog, a monkey,
and a viper. The sack was then thrown into a deep river,
where the entire panicked menagerie would drown. Other
prisoners were fed to wild beasts or dragged behind stamped-
ing horses in the coliseum for the entertainment of spectators.

The most shameful way for a person to be executed in
first-century Rome was crucifixion. The Roman orator
Cicero described it as "the most cruel and atrocious of pun-
ishments." A prisoner sentenced to crucifixion was stripped
naked and nailed through the wrists to the beam of a wooden
cross. When the cross was raised, the person's entire body
weight was supported by the arms, which often resulted in
dislocated elbows and shoulders. Breathing became difficult

due to the inordinate pressure of the body's weight upon the lungs. Some prisoners hung that way for days until they finally suffocated, starved, or died of dehydration.

To further the humiliation, crucifixions took place by the side of major thoroughfares so that travelers and passersby could witness the prisoners' suffering. After death, the condemned were denied a proper burial. Their corpses were left suspended for the birds to pick clean. Is it any wonder that the English word excruciating derives from the Latin word for "cross"?

J ared had spent hours as a child exploring Jerusalem. It was difficult for his family to make the long journey there from Tyre three times every year, but they had made a point to celebrate every Passover in the capital city . . . until the senseless death of their dad's brother Caleb. When Jared's family wasn't offering sacrifices at the temple or preparing for a feast, he had investigated every street and market, every garden and gate, and every road and pool, inside and out-side Jerusalem's walls. Sometimes his adventures involved his grandfather, father, brothers, or friends from his caravan; other times his adventures involved no one but himself.

Only one area of the city had been forbidden to him: the Gennath Gate on the west side. The gate opened to a well-traveled highway that ran from Shechem in the north to Hebron and Beersheba in the south. Not far from the gate lay a lush garden and a well-kept cemetery. The vista beyond the gate was breathtaking, especially at sunset.

Yet Jared's parents would not allow him or his brothers to venture near it. Jared was nine years old when he discovered why. He and Noam had made a game of racing from gate to gate around the interior of the city. They started at the Valley Gate on the east side, raced down to the Water Gate and then west to the Essene Gate. They both knew that the Gennath Gate was next, but neither wanted to end their game. So they ran past the high priest's residence, past Herod's Palace, and past the towers of Mariamne, Phasael, and Hippicus. Noam reached the gate first, but Jared was the first to exit the city through it. On the north side of the road, just outside the gate, lay the Towers Pool. Jared walked past it, and Noam followed—warning his brother every step of the way about what would happen if their parents found out where they were.

The terrain beyond the pool was rocky and hilly. Several large vertical poles rose from the ground like limbless trees. Jared estimated that if he climbed to the top of one of them, he could see the temple. As they got closer to the poles, they saw birds—dozens of them. When the birds scattered, they saw carcasses. Corpses, many of which were attached to wooden beams, lay in grotesque poses on the hillside.

The place, as they later learned, was called Golgotha. Jared and Noam stared at the tableau with a queasy fascination and then hurried back to a more familiar part of the city before anyone saw them. Neither of them ever spoke of the incident—not even to one another.

Jared witnessed his first crucifixion two years later at the same spot. A man his father knew had been arrested for killing two tax collectors and returning money to several Jewish families. His execution also had taken place during the Passover festival.

Jared's father deemed his sons old enough to take with him to pay his respects to the man. By the time they arrived at Golgotha, his cross was already aloft, and he had lost his foothold. His body sagged and his arms stretched far beyond their normal length. His strangled moans grew louder as he struggled to take a breath. He twisted and turned his body, trying to get some kind of leverage, some way to take the pressure off his lungs. If he ever saw Jared's father, he gave no indication of it.

Jared and his brothers stayed at Golgotha only for a moment that day, but the scene stayed with Jared for the rest of his life. He recalled it now as he stood mere steps from where the man had been suspended.

A cadre of Roman soldiers and servants were gathered a short distance away, preparing pulleys, ropes, and ladders near three of the vertical posts. One of the soldiers swore when he noticed his own blood on the tool he was holding.

"A man who gathers vines from a thorn bush should expect to bleed," his fellow soldier taunted.

"The king of the Jews needed a crown," the first soldier explained with a laugh.

Both men looked in the direction of Jared and his brothers. They motioned toward other soldiers standing nearby and pointed at the brothers.

"They think we're disciples of Jesus," Jared whispered to his brothers.

"If we were, we'd be the only ones here," Seth grumbled. "If his followers cannot be found at his crucifixion, what hope is there for recruiting them to support us against the Romans?"

The soldiers spoke to one another in loud voices about flogging the prisoner from Galilee—the one who would not speak or cry out, no matter how many times the metal-studded whip tore open the skin on his back.

"I treated him like a king," one of the soldiers called with mock sincerity. "I placed a royal robe on his shoulders and gave him a scepter."

"You *beat* him with his scepter," another soldier corrected him.

"I kneeled before him."

"And then spit in his face."

Both men laughed and returned to their work. Jared and his brothers walked back toward Pilate's residence.

On the way, they were met by a large crowd moving slowly toward them. At the center of the crowd was Jesus of Nazareth, though even his closest friends—wherever they were—would have had difficulty recognizing him. His face was swollen and misshapen. Blood matted his hair. The large wooden beam that rested across his shoulders threatened to topple him. His steps were lurching and uncertain; each one brought a wince of pain to his eyes.

When the group got closer, one of the soldiers walking next to Jesus pointed in the brothers' direction. "Take up his cross," he commanded.

Before Jared could ask which of the three he was talking to, a man walking just behind them stepped over to Jesus and lifted the cross beam from his shoulders. The exhausted Galilean offered him a look of gratitude.

The man carried the beam the short distance to Golgotha. He was followed by Jesus and his Roman guards; the Jewish priests, elders, and teachers of the law who had brought the charges of blasphemy against him; and an assortment of grieving followers, curious passersby, and locals eager to see a crucifixion. Bringing up the rear were a dozen or more women, several of whom were weeping loudly.

As the procession reached the Gennath Gate, Jesus turned to them, and in a surprisingly robust voice, said, "Daughters of Jerusalem, do not weep for me, but weep for yourselves and for your children. For behold, the days are coming when they will say, 'Blessed are the barren and the wombs that never bore and the breasts that never nursed!' Then they will begin to say to the mountains, 'Fall on us,' and to the hills, 'Cover us.' For if they do these things when the wood is green, what will happen when it is dry?"

The Roman soldiers looked at one another in confusion. The Jewish religious leaders exchanged outraged exclamations. Jared recognized one of them as the leader of the arrest party in the olive grove and the man who frightened Simon Peter away from the high priest's courtyard. The women whispered among themselves.

At Golgotha, the man pressed into service by the Romans dropped the cross beam and hurried back to the city. The soldiers and servants positioned the beam and readied their tools. Jesus struggled to stay upright. The Jewish religious leaders claimed the prime spot for watching the execution: the center of the hill, directly in front of the middle of the three crosses that would be raised that day. Other witnesses filled in the hillside. The women made their way to a rocky outcropping some distance away from the cross.

Jared and his brothers stood behind the Jewish leaders. The busy road leading to and from the Gennath Gate lay just behind them—so close that they could hear the comments of passersby.

A soldier offered Jesus a cup of wine mixed with myrrh. Jesus took a small sip and handed the cup back. His hand trembled.

"Why does he refuse the drink?" Seth asked. "It will ease his pain." Neither of his brothers offered an answer.

The soldiers stripped Jesus of his clothes. His blood had soaked through not only his inner garment, but also his outer one. Several people in the crowd gasped when they saw the open wounds on Jesus's back.

"Have they never witnessed a flogging before?" Seth whispered.

The soldier who had offered Jesus the drink suddenly pushed him down. He didn't have to push hard. Jesus landed on his back on the rocky ground. He groaned, as did his sympathizers in the crowd.

Two soldiers dragged him by the arms and positioned his shoulders on the crossbeam. They stretched out his arms and held them in place while two other soldiers, holding hammers and heavy wrought-iron nails, kneeled over Jesus's hands. With measured and precise blows, they drove the nails through Jesus's wrists. Servants using ropes and pulleys lifted the cross beam, with Jesus on it, to the tall vertical post. Other servants standing on ladders quickly attached the two pieces of the cross. When their work was finished, they moved their equipment to the next cross and left Jesus suspended between heaven and earth.

The vertical beam of Jesus's cross had a narrow ledge about halfway up the area where the prisoner's body would be positioned. The ridge offered a small bit of leverage on which the condemned man could support himself. That leverage reduced the weight the nails in his wrists had to support, but it could also extend the time it took the victim to die.

The Romans went one step further with Jesus. As he hung from the cross, they bent his legs slightly and positioned his feet one over the other. They drove a nail through his heels, giving him an excruciating second source of leverage.

Jared watched Jesus intently as he struggled to maneuver himself into a position that didn't cause him blinding pain. Meanwhile, the Roman soldiers and their servants raised two other men, one on either side of Jesus, to their crosses.

According to the signs above their heads, the two men were robbers. Jared and his brothers recognized them as insurrectionists but had not had much contact with them. The sign above Jesus's head read, "This is Jesus, the king of the Jews."

Jesus's accusers reacted immediately to the sign. Jared watched as they huddled together, gesturing wildly and pointing to Jesus's cross.

"This cannot be," one of the priests seethed. "Pilate must be told to change the wording." Three others volunteered to convey the group's displeasure in an official capacity. But before they could even *turn* toward the Roman governor's residence, the sky suddenly grew dark, as before a spring storm. The men stopped. Everyone at Golgotha at that moment, from the soldiers and servants, to the priests and women, to the criminals on either side of Jesus, looked to the sky. There were no clouds on the horizon.

A sense of unease settled over the crowd.

"Father, forgive them, for they know not what they do." With considerable effort and obvious pain, Jesus looked around at the witnesses to his execution. Jared saw no anger or malice in his eyes, and he wondered if the Galilean had drunk the myrrh wine after all.

Jesus's words were followed by the raucous laughter of Roman soldiers kneeling at the base of his cross. They were casting lots for Jesus's only possessions: his clothes. One centurion walked away with his belt and sandals. Two others took his head covering and his bloodstained outer garment. One even took his inner garment, whose stains would likely *never* come out.

Whatever pity Jared felt for the teacher from Nazareth vanished at that moment. After all, their common enemy remained, and Jesus—who held such power and potential—had done nothing to rid Israel of the Roman occupation.

"You had many thousands following you," he muttered. "They could have made you king, if you had given the word."

His voice grew louder. "You accomplished nothing! Your followers stand here to watch you die! What would you have them do now?"

From the road behind him, a man yelled, "You who would destroy the temple and rebuild it in three days, save yourself! If you are the Son of God, come down from the cross!" A chorus of laughter and a barrage of other insults followed. Jared's words were lost among them.

In front of him someone shouted, "He saved others; he cannot save himself. He is the King of Israel; let him come down from the cross, and we will believe in him. He trusts in God; let God deliver him now, if he desires him."

The leader of the arrest party has found his voice, Jared observed.

The robber hanging next to Jesus on his left joined the verbal assault. "Aren't you the Christ?" he cried. "Save yourself and us!"

Jesus offered no defense of himself or rebuke of his mockers. That was left to perhaps the least likely person present.

"Do you not fear God, since you are under the same sentence of condemnation?" the other robber asked. "And we indeed justly, for we are receiving the due reward of our deeds; but this man has done nothing wrong." He turned his head as far as he could and looked at the teacher from Nazareth. "Jesus, remember me when you come into your kingdom."

"Truly, I say to you, today you will be with me in paradise," Jesus replied. Jared noticed that the Galilean's voice was growing weaker.

A small group of men and women made their way to the foot of Jesus's cross. The Roman centurion guarding it eyed them cautiously but did not stop them. One of the women trembled as she gazed at the Galilean's agony up close.

"That is his mother," one of the teachers of the law whispered.

Jesus looked down at the woman and then at a young man standing near her. Jared thought he recognized the man from the olive grove, but he couldn't be sure. "Woman, behold, your son!" Jesus said. He pushed himself up using the leverage from the nail in his feet and took several deep breaths before lowering himself again.

He turned to the young man and said, "Behold, your mother!" Jared stepped forward and took a long look at the disciple whom Jesus must have trusted implicitly.

A lull settled over the crowd. The curiosity seekers wandered away, as did a number of the priests, teachers, and elders. It was Preparation Day; the Sabbath would begin at sundown, and there was work to be done. Death from cruci-fixion rarely happened quickly; most prisoners suffered for hours and even days before the weight of their organs crushed their lungs and left them unable to breathe. Jared's brothers looked at him to see if he wanted to leave too. He shook his head at their silent question and thought, "What motivates such a man?" His silence reflected his inward thoughts about how different Jesus was from himself and his own ambitions.

Jesus's voice cut though the silence. "*Eli, Eli, lema sabach-thani?*" he cried.

"This man is calling Elijah," Seth said. Others in the crowd heard him and passed on his explanation.

The man who led Jesus's arrest party turned and looked at the brothers as if they were Samaritans. Correcting Seth, he explained, "He said, 'My God, my God, why have you forsaken me?'" He spat his words as though they were distasteful.

"I thirst." Everyone in the crowd looked up at Jesus. His voice was little more than a croak.

One of the soldiers opened his pack and pulled out a jug of wine vinegar, the sour wine preferred by the Roman army during their foreign campaigns. He poured some into a sponge and used a stick to lift it to Jesus's lips.

Someone in the back of the crowd yelled, "Wait, let us see whether Elijah will come to save him." Jared and Noam looked at Seth and shook their heads. Jared started to say something but was interrupted.

"It is finished," Jesus announced. His head dropped for-ward so that his chin was resting on his chest.

A tremor shook the ground of Golgotha. The three crosses swayed as though they were being blown by a storm. Small rocks rolled down the side of the hill. The witnesses who remained exchanged uneasy glances.

A Roman centurion who stood guard over Jesus placed his hand on the cross to steady himself. "Truly this was the Son of God!" he said.

The priests and their associates whispered their outrage to one another but said nothing aloud.

Moments later, the delegation that had gone to talk to Pilate returned. The men looked at Jesus and the two who were crucified with him. "Their bodies must not be left to hang during the Sabbath," they announced. "Pilate has issued orders to break the prisoners' legs."

The Roman centurion nodded to one of his men, who picked up a large iron bar. With several violent but well-aimed swings, he broke the legs of the robbers on either side of Jesus. Their bodies slumped, and they began to struggle for breath. Several agonizing moments later, both were dead.

The soldier lifted the bar to break Jesus's legs but saw that the Galilean already was dead. He nodded to a second soldier, who drove his spear through the dead man's side. A mixture of blood and water poured from the wound.

Jared and his brothers turned to leave just as two well-dressed men arrived at the scene. Jared recognized one of them from the high priest's courtyard. The two men approached the centurion guard with unusual boldness. One of them pointed to Jesus.

"Pilate has released this man's body to me," he said. His tone did not leave room for argument.

"Joseph! Nicodemus! What is the meaning of this?" It was the leader of the arrest party, the one with whom Joseph had quarreled hours earlier.

Jared told his brothers to go on without him. His curiosity was piqued. In the nearby garden, he saw servants pulling a cart loaded with what looked to be jars of perfume and strips of linen.

"Eli, I am here to claim this man's body," Joseph replied.

"This man was a blasphemer," Eli said. The disgust in his voice was unmistakable. "He has been crucified as a common criminal. Leave his carcass to the animals and birds."

"The hour grows late," Nicodemus replied. "We have much work to do and no time to discuss this matter with you."

The soldiers ordered the servants to take down Jesus's body and carry it to the nearby garden. Joseph and Nicodemus followed them without giving their colleagues a second glance.

Eli and his companions looked at one another, shook their heads, and departed. Jared guessed that they would be discussing the matter long into the Sabbath.

Jared wandered over to the garden and found a secluded spot behind a shrub. He watched as Joseph, Nicodemus, and their servants worked quickly inside a tomb that appeared to be newly cut. Jesus's body was laid on a bench carved from the stone inside the tomb. The men covered the corpse with myrrh and aloe. ("Seventy-five pounds worth," according to

Nicodemus.) After all the perfume had been applied, they wrapped the body tightly with strips of linen.

Their final task was to roll a large, disc-shaped stone into place in front of the tomb. The stone was set in a sloped channel that made rolling it downhill into place easy, but rolling it away extremely difficult.

Sundown was approaching, so the men hurried away. Not one of them noticed the curious and confused onlooker.

The curious onlooker, in turn, didn't notice that all of them were being watched by a group of women in an even more secluded spot.

Chapter 12

The Legacy
Jesus Knew

THE FUTURE OF ROME AND
CHRISTIANITY IN 1ST CENTURY AD

Three entities collided in the mid-first century: the venerable nation of Israel, the mighty Roman Empire, and a small sect of passionate Jews who followed a man they believed to be the Messiah. Who would have guessed that when the dust of history settled, the small sect—later to be known as The Way and eventually the Christian church—would leave a worldwide imprint in the two thousand years that followed?

After Jesus's death, Israel continued to chafe under Roman authority. Rebellions large and small created fissures in the relationship between Rome and Israel. Temple priests stopped offering sacrifices on behalf of the emperor. Factions of Jewish political groups continued their assaults on Roman institutions. Many Jewish citizens refused to pay the burdensome taxes demanded by Rome.

Rome retaliated in AD 70. The Roman army, led by Titus, conquered Jerusalem and destroyed Herod's temple. The people of Israel were exiled. Thus the Jewish people were scattered throughout the world, once again with no nation of their own. A would-be Messiah named Bar Kokhba led a Jewish revolt against Rome in AD 132 that resulted in the deaths of tens of thousands of Roman soldiers and hundreds of thousands of Jewish rebels.

When the Roman Empire split in AD 286, the land of Israel fell under Byzantine control until AD 636, when Muslim Arabs captured the region. Caliph Abd al-Malik built a Muslim mosque, the Dome of the Rock, on the site of the former Jewish temple. European Christian Crusaders, urged on by Pope Urban II, captured Palestine in 1099 and massacred its Muslim inhabitants. The region was recaptured by the Mamluks in 1291. In 1516, it fell under the control of the Ottoman Empire, where it stayed for the next four hundred years. In the wake of World War I, Great Britain assumed control of the region and talk began of reestablishing a Jewish nation in Palestine. It took until 1948 for Israel to become an official, recognized country, and Jews from around the world have migrated there to make it their home.

The Roman Empire faced a different trajectory. It grew in power and size for another century after Jesus's death. By AD 117, it encompassed Europe, Asia Minor, and North Africa. The decline began shortly thereafter. In AD 286, the political behemoth split into the Western Empire and the Eastern (or Byzantine) Empire, each with its own emperor. The Western Empire was beset by invasions from barbarians, including the Vandals and Visigoths. The city of Rome was sacked on several occasions. In AD 476, the Western Empire fell to the Germanic commander Odoacer. The Byzantine Empire endured, although with curtailed power and influence, for almost another millennium. In 1453, Ottoman forces conquered the capital city of Constantinople (which they later renamed Istanbul), effectively ending the Roman Empire.

Christianity grew exponentially in the years following Jesus's crucifixion. His followers, emboldened by reports of his resurrection, spread his message throughout Judea and Galilee. The apostle Paul and other missionaries carried the news of Jesus to the farthest reaches of the Roman Empire and beyond. They started churches in the places they visited to nurture their converts and help them grow in their faith.

Roman officials found much to fear in the sect known as The Way, and started a campaign of intense persecution against Christians. According to tradition, all but one (John) of Jesus's apostles was martyred. The persecution lasted more than 250 years, until Emperor Galerius put an end to it in AD 311. His successor, Constantine, who professed Christianity himself, legalized Christian worship two years later. Theodosius I named Christianity the official state religion in AD 380. Three hundred and fifty years after it began, the small sect that coalesced in response to the teachings and example of Jesus of Nazareth had "conquered" Rome.

Today, more than two billion people—nearly one-third of the earth's population—identify themselves as Christians.

S ilence and tears marked the beginning of the Sabbath in Phyllis's home.

The small group of women who gathered there found little peace or comfort on their day of rest and reflection. Every conversation—every *pause* in conversation—seemed to trigger new, visceral reactions to Jesus's crucifixion.

Chana cried with her friends but felt helpless to comfort them. The ache she felt, after knowing Jesus only a few days, nearly overwhelmed her. The lines of pain and sorrow on *their* faces were etched from years of following him and sitting at his feet. Chana could not imagine their sense of loss.

The restrictions of the Sabbath left them more time to dwell on the circumstances of Jesus's arrest and crucifixion. They were prohibited from baking bread, spinning thread, sewing stitches, or washing their wool clothes. Ordinarily the women eagerly anticipated the Sabbath and the respite it provided. These were not ordinary times.

As the silences grew, so did the discomfort. None of the women dared to ask what Jesus's death meant for their lives beyond that day. In the quiet of the Sabbath morning, Chana thought about how fortune had favored her friends. She imagined the conversations they shared with Jesus, the miracles they witnessed, the teachings they heard. The words were out of her mouth before she knew they were coming.

"Tell me about Jesus."

The other women stirred from their private mourning and looked at one another. They all started to speak at once and then laughed through their tears. Phyllis stood and walked to the window. "I think about his parables," she said.

Those five words opened the floodgates.

Phyllis described the crowds that pressed in to hear him in Galilee, and she recalled Jesus's parable of the wayward son in vivid detail. No sooner had she finished speaking than another woman shared the parable of the lost coin. A third woman laughed as she spoke of struggling to understand Jesus's parable of the mustard seed.

Chana was an eager pupil. She absorbed their words like a sponge. She pressed each woman for more details. She probed the recesses of their memories. She hung on each new recollection. The more she heard, the more she wanted to hear—about Jesus's rejection by the people in his hometown, about his kindness to the Samaritan woman, about his love for children, about his desire to be alone after a busy day.

Story after story poured forth. Phyllis and two other women managed to pull themselves away long enough to serve the morning meal: flatbread and a lentil stew that had been prepared the day before and packed in straw to maintain warmth.

In the early afternoon, the women climbed the stairs to the roof. The conversation never abated. One woman would speak for a while and then yield to the next. Sometimes two or more would share their recollections of the same event. Chana marveled over how their experiences were similar yet unique. Each new speaker seemed to bring a different slant to the story.

By the time the sun completed its journey to the western horizon, Chana's friends had talked themselves hoarse. Phyllis pointed at the evening sky. "I see three stars," she said. "The Sabbath has ended."

The women exchanged sheepish smiles as they made their way to the staircase. Chana wondered if any of them had ever spoken so many words in a single day. On her way down the stairs, Phyllis offered one more observation.

"Look at the happiness we've found telling Chana about Jesus."

The Sabbath conversation in Uri's home was not nearly as long—or as polite—as the one in Phyllis's. Uri's guests wrapped their bread around onions and leeks and dipped it in olive oil. They dined on dried figs and pomegranates. They drank newly fermented wine whose sweetness was cut with water.

And they argued.

At the center of the verbal sparring was Jared, who still longed to resist Rome. Noam and Seth backed their brother, but Jared could tell they were doing it out of loyalty and not because they truly agreed with him. He seemed to be quite alone in his belief among the men gathered on Uri's rooftop.

"Jesus of Nazareth united Judeans and Galileans in his cause, just as we hope to do." Jared pointed to a few Judeans and a few Galileans in the group to drive home his point.

"He united them and taught them to turn their other cheeks to their enemies after they've been struck," one of the Galileans grumbled.

"He told them that if a Roman soldier forces them to carry his equipment for a mile, they should carry it for an extra mile as well," one of the Judeans added. The comment immediately triggered Jared's memories of his uncle Caleb, but he struggled not to reveal his inner pain . . . or any emotion. "What you say is true," he acknowledged. "But that was before they saw what their enemies are capable of. Won't their anger now burn toward the soldiers who mocked and crucified their leader? Won't *our* enemies become *their* enemies?"

"Haven't they been told to *love* their enemies?" Uri countered.

"The one who gave them those orders now lies dead by his enemy's hand—by *our* enemy's hand," Jared pointed out. "Will they forget the sight of their messiah crucified like a runaway slave?"

A second Judean spoke up. "They watched their messiah's arrest in the olive grove and cut off a single ear. They watched while he was dragged before Pilate and did nothing. They watched him being beaten and did nothing. They watched as he was nailed to a cross and did nothing. Now they've gone into hiding. They fear for their own lives. And still you have hope that they will do *something.*"

"You saw the crowds that welcomed him to Jerusalem but a week ago. You heard how the people cheered and cried for him," Jared reminded his companions. "What if he had marched not to the temple that day but to the Antonia Fortress? Would those crowds not have followed him? Would they not have done whatever he asked of them?"

"That spirit has since departed them."

"It can be found again," Jared insisted. "If we sow a hatred of our common enemies—Roman leaders—then we may turn their passion against those enemies. I am convinced that they can be persuaded."

No one cheered or cried for Jared. Instead, his words were met with skepticism and doubt. Their greater concern was the internal clash among Jewish leaders.

Uri seemed to sum up the feelings of the entire group when he asked, "How will they find a spirit of courage again? What could possibly give them the boldness you speak of?"

Jared offered no reply.

The day after Jesus's death, many of the chief priests and elders seemed more vexed than they'd been when the Galilean was alive. They asked Eli to repeat the words he heard Jesus say about rising from the dead. The request surprised Eli; he assumed he'd been invited to the temple to receive congratulations for ridding Judah of the blasphemer from Galilee.

Eli did as he was asked, faithfully recounting every word he could remember. When he finished, he posed a question of his own. "Are you concerned that he *will* rise from the dead?"

One priest jumped to his feet and walked away to show his disgust at the very implication of the question. "We are concerned about the Galilean's *disciples*," a second priest explained. "They may have an agenda of their own. Now that the matter of the imposter has been settled, we must not suffer a final embarrassment at the hands of his followers."

Eli shook his head. "The bravest of his followers fled like a frightened rabbit when I recognized him in the courtyard," he said. "Jesus of Nazareth's disciples are not men we should concern ourselves with."

The chief priests and elders disagreed, and the distance from the temple to Pilate's residence was well within a Sabbath's day journey. That's why, just hours after Jesus's crucifixion, Eli found himself once again in the presence of the Roman governor outside Herod's palace with a retinue from the temple.

"Sir," Eli said to him, "we remember how that impostor said, while he was still alive, 'After three days I will rise.' Therefore, order the tomb to be made secure until the third day, lest his disciples go and steal him away and tell the people, 'He has risen from the dead,' and the last fraud will be worse than the first."

Pilate considered his words for a moment. "You have a guard of soldiers," he told Eli. "Go, make it as secure as you can."

A small squadron of soldiers followed Eli and his companions to the garden tomb where Joseph and Nicodemus had laid the Galilean's body. (One of the companions was a servant of Joseph who had helped prepare the body.) The soldiers placed a seal on the stone that covered the tomb and posted a guard in front of it. Other guards were dispatched to various parts of the garden.

"The tomb is your responsibility," one of the priests reminded Eli as they walked back to the temple. "Pray that it is not disturbed."

"Let the responsibility fall on me," Eli replied. He didn't bother to feign humility. "Who would disturb the grave of a crucified criminal, much less one with a Roman guard posted in front of it? Mark my words: we will hear no more of this matter. By the next Passover, the words and work of the Galilean will be long forgotten, and his followers will be scattered to the winds."

The next morning, Chana rose early, before Phyllis or anyone else in the house stirred, and went for a walk. The stories and recollections from the previous day swirled through her mind. She needed to sort through them, to make sense of what she heard, to try to understand Jesus as her friends did. She thought of a place where she could be alone with her thoughts: a garden spot near Jesus's tomb.

As she neared the Gennath Gate, however, darker memories pushed their way into her thoughts. She felt a tightness in the pit of her stomach. Tears welled in her eyes. *The pain he must have felt as he passed through this very gate.*

Her thoughts were interrupted by a shout from the nearly empty street behind her and then an excited cry:

"He is risen!"

She turned to see Mary Magdalene rushing toward her. "He is risen!" she repeated. A torrent of breathless words followed. "I told Simon Peter and the others. They ran all the way there, but they'll find nothing because he's not there. I was on my way to tell others when I saw you."

Chana had never seen anyone so excited. She wanted to share Mary's elation, but her confusion wouldn't allow it. Was she talking about John or one of the other disciples—perhaps someone was sick? Why was his early awakening cause for such excitement?

Mary recognized her confusion. She took a deep breath, grabbed Chana's hands, and looked her in the eyes.

"Jesus," she said. "He is risen!"

IF YOU ENJOYED THIS BOOK, WILL YOU CONSIDER SHARING THE MESSAGE WITH OTHERS?

Mention the book in a blog post or through Facebook, Twitter, Pinterest, or upload a picture through Instagram.

Recommend this book to those in your small group, book club, workplace, and classes.

Head over to facebook.com/WorthyPublishing, "LIKE" the page, and post a comment as to what you enjoyed the most.

Tweet "I recommend reading #TheWorldJesusKnew from @MuseumofBible // @WorthyPub"

Pick up a copy for someone you know who would be challenged and encouraged by this message.

Write a book review online.

Visit us at worthypublishing.com

twitter.com/worthypub

worthypub.tumblr.com

facebook.com/worthypublishing

pinterest.com/worthypub

instagram.com/worthypub

youtube.com/worthypublishing

museum of the Bible

Experience the Book that Shapes History

Museum of the Bible is a 430,000-square-foot building located in the heart of Washington, D.C.—just steps from the National Mall and the U.S. Capitol. Displaying artifacts from several collections, the Museum explores the Bible's history, narrative and impact through high-tech exhibits, immersive settings, and interactive experiences. Upon entering, you will pass through two massive, bronze gates resembling printing plates from Genesis 1. Beyond the gates, an incredible replica of an ancient artifact containing Psalm 19 hangs behind etched glass panels. Come be inspired by the imagination and innovation used to display thousands of years of biblical history.

Museum of the Bible aims to be the most technologically advanced museum in the world, starting with its unique Digital Guide that allows guests to personalize their museum experience with navigation, customized tours, supplemental visual and audio content, and more.

For more information and to plan your visit, go to museumoftheBible.org.